HV875 .A3186 2009

Adoption

DATE DUE

MAR 2 4	
JAN 0 3 2010	
DEC 1 1 2010	
11 Dec 2015	
FLL Mar 2020	
DISCARDED	

DEMCO, INC. 38-2931

INTRODUCING
ISSUES WITH
OPPOSING
VIEWPOINTS®

Adoption

Noël Merino, *Book Editor*

GREENHAVEN PRESS
A part of Gale, Cengage Learning

GALE
CENGAGE Learning™

Detroit • New York • San Francisco • New Haven, Conn • Waterville, Maine • London

Christine Nasso, *Publisher*
Elizabeth Des Chenes, *Managing Editor*

© 2009 Greenhaven Press, a part of Gale, Cengage Learning

Gale and Greenhaven Press are registered trademarks used herein under license.

For more information, contact:
Greenhaven Press
27500 Drake Rd.
Farmington Hills, MI 48331-3535
Or you can visit our Internet site at gale.cengage.com

ALL RIGHTS RESERVED.
No part of this work covered by the copyright herein may be reproduced, transmitted, stored, or used in any form or by any means graphic, electronic, or mechanical, including but not limited to photocopying, recording, scanning, digitizing, taping, Web distribution, information networks, or information storage and retrieval systems, except as permitted under Section 107 or 108 of the 1976 United States Copyright Act, without the prior written permission of the publisher.

For product information and technology assistance, contact us at

Gale Customer Support, 1-800-877-4253
For permission to use material from this text or product, submit all requests online at www.cengage.com/permissions

Further permissions questions can be emailed to permissionrequest@cengage.com

Articles in Greenhaven Press anthologies are often edited for length to meet page requirements. In addition, original titles of these works are changed to clearly present the main thesis and to explicitly indicate the author's opinion. Every effort is made to ensure that Greenhaven Press accurately reflects the original intent of the authors. Every effort has been made to trace the owners of copyrighted material.

Cover image copyright Thomas M. Perkins, 2008. Used under license from Shutterstock.com.

LIBRARY OF CONGRESS CATALOGING-IN-PUBLICATION DATA

Adoption / Noël Merino, book editor.
    p. cm. — (Introducing issues with opposing viewpoints)
Includes bibliographical references and index.
ISBN 978-0-7377-4165-0 (hardcover)
1. Adoption—Juvenile literature. I. Merino, Noël.
HV875.A3427 2009
362.734—dc22

                                                              2008031371

Printed in the United States of America
1 2 3 4 5 6 7 12 11 10 09 08

Contents

Foreword

I ndulging in a wide spectrum of ideas, beliefs, and perspectives is a critical cornerstone of democracy. After all, it is often debates over differences of opinion, such as whether to legalize abortion, how to treat prisoners, or when to enact the death penalty, that shape our society and drive it forward. Such diversity of thought is frequently regarded as the hallmark of a healthy and civilized culture. As the Reverend Clifford Schutjer of the First Congregational Church in Mansfield, Ohio, declared in a 2001 sermon, "Surrounding oneself with only like-minded people, restricting what we listen to or read only to what we find agreeable is irresponsible. Refusing to entertain doubts once we make up our minds is a subtle but deadly form of arrogance." With this advice in mind, Introducing Issues with Opposing Viewpoints books aim to open readers' minds to the critically divergent views that comprise our world's most important debates.

Introducing Issues with Opposing Viewpoints simplifies for students the enormous and often overwhelming mass of material now available via print and electronic media. Collected in every volume is an array of opinions that captures the essence of a particular controversy or topic. Introducing Issues with Opposing Viewpoints books embody the spirit of nineteenth-century journalist Charles A. Dana's axiom: "Fight for your opinions, but do not believe that they contain the whole truth, or the only truth." Absorbing such contrasting opinions teaches students to analyze the strength of an argument and compare it to its opposition. From this process readers can inform and strengthen their own opinions, or be exposed to new information that will change their minds. Introducing Issues with Opposing Viewpoints is a mosaic of different voices. The authors are statesmen, pundits, academics, journalists, corporations, and ordinary people who have felt compelled to share their experiences and ideas in a public forum. Their words have been collected from newspapers, journals, books, speeches, interviews, and the Internet, the fastest growing body of opinionated material in the world.

Introducing Issues with Opposing Viewpoints shares many of the well-known features of its critically acclaimed parent series, Opposing Viewpoints. The articles are presented in a pro/con format, allowing readers to absorb divergent perspectives side by side. Active reading questions preface each viewpoint, requiring the student to approach the material thoughtfully and carefully. Useful charts, graphs, and cartoons supplement each article. A thorough introduction provides readers with crucial background on an issue. An annotated bibliography points the reader toward articles, books, and Web sites that contain additional information on the topic. An appendix of organizations to contact contains a wide variety of charities, nonprofit organizations, political groups, and private enterprises that each hold a position on the issue at hand. Finally, a comprehensive index allows readers to locate content quickly and efficiently.

Introducing Issues with Opposing Viewpoints is also significantly different from Opposing Viewpoints. As the series title implies, its presentation will help introduce students to the concept of opposing viewpoints and learn to use this material to aid in critical writing and debate. The series' four-color, accessible format makes the books attractive and inviting to readers of all levels. In addition, each viewpoint has been carefully edited to maximize a reader's understanding of the content. Short but thorough viewpoints capture the essence of an argument. A substantial, thought-provoking essay question placed at the end of each viewpoint asks the student to further investigate the issues raised in the viewpoint, compare and contrast two authors' arguments, or consider how one might go about forming an opinion on the topic at hand. Each viewpoint contains sidebars that include at-a-glance information and handy statistics. A Facts About section located in the back of the book further supplies students with relevant facts and figures.

Following in the tradition of the Opposing Viewpoints series, Greenhaven Press continues to provide readers with invaluable exposure to the controversial issues that shape our world. As John Stuart Mill once wrote: "The only way in which a human being can make some approach to knowing the whole of a subject is by hearing what can be said about it by persons of every variety of opinion and studying all modes in which it can be looked at by every character of mind. No wise man ever acquired his wisdom in any mode but this." It is to this principle that Introducing Issues with Opposing Viewpoints books are dedicated.

Introduction

"Adoption is not about finding children for families, but about finding families for children."

—Joyce Maguire Pavao, *The Family of Adoption*

Perhaps part of the reason that international adoption has become a topic of public debate in recent years is due to the highly publicized international adoptions of movie stars such as Angelina Jolie and Brad Pitt. Angelina Jolie adopted her first child, Maddox, a seven-month-old Cambodian boy, with her then-husband Billy Bob Thornton in 2001. In July 2005 she adopted a six-month-old girl from Ethiopia named Zahara. In December 2005 Brad Pitt, not married to Jolie, adopted both children as well. In 2006 Jolie gave birth to her and Pitt's child, Shiloh, and less than a year later the couple adopted a fourth child, Pax, a three-year-old boy from Vietnam. Jolie is expecting twins with father Pitt, due in mid-2008.

The adoptions of Jolie and Pitt have caused a public debate about international adoption. There has been controversy about the adoption of Jolie's first child, Maddox. Lynn Devin, the former owner of Seattle International Adoptions, pled guilty to making false claims that some of the children whose adoptions the agency handled were orphans. The FBI closed down the agency, the same one that Jolie used to adopt Maddox. The controversy has led some to speculate that Maddox may have not been an orphan, as Jolie was told. Adam Pertman of the Evan B. Donaldson Adoption Institute says that there had been concerns about adoptions in Cambodia, including concerns about "baby-selling, coercion and more subtle ways of inducing women to give up their babies." This kind of fraud in international adoption has led some to lament that Jolie did not use the opportunity to speak out on the issue: "Angelina is *not* a hero in the adoption community," said Tatiana Beams, a Seattle-based international adoption advocate. "It would be nice to see her speak out on issues and policies surrounding international adoption."

Concerns about adoption agencies giving fraudulent information also surfaced in response to Jolie's second adopted child. The adoption agency that processed that adoption, Wide Horizons for Children, had reported that Zahara's mother had died from AIDS. Zahara's mother, Mentewab Dawit, came forward to the press later. While not wanting Zahara back and not disputing the adoption, Dawit is upset that Jolie was told that Zahara's mother was dead: "I'm happy to see my daughter in a better life, in a better place. The thing that makes me upset is that Angelina is saying I'm dead—I'm alive and have never had AIDS."

Jolie's third adopted child also has caused controversy. Pax's mother was reportedly a heroin addict and Pax's grandparents signed the papers relinquishing custody of Pax (causing some to speculate that Pax's mother, Pham Thu Dung, who abandoned the boy two days after giving birth, might surface at some point and contest the adoption). The adoption seemed to happen quickly, causing some to speculate that Jolie had used her fame or money to facilitate a quick adoption. There is no indication that these charges are true: Heidi Gonzalez, Vietnam program adoption coordinator of Adoptions from the Heart, a nonprofit adoption agency used by Jolie for Pax's adoption, said that Jolie "received no preferential treatment from the Vietnamese government" and that "her application was not fast-tracked." In addition, Gonzalez confirmed that no money had been donated by Jolie to Pax's Vietnamese orphanage in order to gain favor, as some had speculated.

A general criticism that has been voiced against Jolie and other celebrities who have adopted internationally is that their high-profile international adoptions are publicity stunts to help their careers. African journalist Simwogerere Kyazze notes, "It's therefore a cocktail of pressures that has turned our continent into a stomping ground for adoption-crazy celebrities—a desire to appear normal; a chance to escape the harsh northern winters on UN-sponsored junkets; and perhaps some mild interest in black people." But there are those who are not cynical about stars or anyone else adopting internationally. Acknowledging that Jolie, in her capacity as the United Nations High Commissioner for Refugees Goodwill Ambassador, has traveled widely to visit refugee camps, Martha Osborne, a fellow adoptive parent, asks, "Why wouldn't we understand her desire, on a much more private level, to make a difference in the lives of the children that she so often witnessed suffering?"

Celebrities and others who adopt internationally have also been criticized for going abroad to adopt, rather than adopting in their own country. According to Sarah Mraz, director of child programs at Wide Horizons for Children, a private, nonprofit adoption and child welfare agency, "the reason these children are placed with international families is because they cannot be cared for in their country of origin." The needs of children abroad, say many, are of no less importance than the needs of children in one's own country. Still, the lack of controls for adoption in many developing countries, and the frequency of fraudulent behavior on the part of adoption agencies and orphanages, does make international adoption fraught with more controversy than adoption within the United States.

The controversy about international adoptions, especially by celebrities, points out some of the key differences of opinion about adoption. Issues surrounding the rights of birth parents, the importance of race and culture, and notions of what creates a family all are relevant to this topic. *Introducing Issues with Opposing Viewpoints: Adoption* explores a variety of viewpoints on the various issues that arise with adoption, such as this one.

Chapter 1

How Should We View Adoption?

Adoption has developed over the years as a positive way to create a family.

Adoption Is a Social Good

Melanie Stetson

"We take in kids that would've had a bad family life, and we can see to it that they don't, and that they have a happy family."

In the following viewpoint Melanie Stetson uses the story of the Gardner family to illustrate her point that adoption is a good experience and a way to contribute positively to society. Beverly and Sam Gardner have four biological children and twelve adopted children, nine of whom have special needs. Their adopted children are black, white, Latina, and biracial. None of that bothered the Gardner family—they simply wanted to do what was best for the children and give each of them a real family. Melanie Stetson is a staff writer for the *Christian Science Monitor.*

AS YOU READ, CONSIDER THE FOLLOWING QUESTIONS:

1. What three kinds of children did the Gardner family adopt that are usually hard to place?
2. How many children are in the Gardner family?
3. How many children are homeschooled?

Beverly and Sam Gardner never thought they'd have 16 kids. But after their four biological children were born, they started adopting—and couldn't stop. Eventually, 12 more children were added to the family. Each one has a story.

The Gardners' Story

"Chip [now 10] was 6 months old when we got him. He'd been put in a book bag, zipped up, and put in the trash," Bev says, explaining the early days of one of her children. He was rescued after the house where he lived caught fire and one of the firemen discovered him in the garbage behind the house.

> ## FAST FACT
>
> According to the U.S. Department of Health and Human Services, there are over one hundred thousand adoptions in the United States each year.

"Johnny [now 12] was 3-1/2 months early because of his mother's drug abuse. She basically abandoned him in the hospital," Bev continues.

The Gardners adopted Johnny, who can't see and had been diagnosed with cerebral palsy, despite warnings from doctors that he might be a "vegetable."

"He definitely is not!" his mother says.

The Gardners' adopted children are black, white, Latina, and biracial. Nine of them have special needs. None of that bothered the Gardners. Neither did predicted problems.

"Once you fall in love with a child, that's your child, and all the fear just goes away," Bev says. "Once we heard the terrible stories, we couldn't say no."

Bev and Sam both come from big families. After three of their biological children arrived prematurely, the couple decided that since they wanted more, they would adopt. They are Caucasian, but were happy to adopt black or biracial children, who are harder to place.

Caring for Special Needs Children

After the Gardners' first two adoptions, they came into contact with state organizations that help find homes for at-risk children. After hearing the stories about these children, the Gardners became foster parents, caring for more than a hundred special-needs children for periods as short as a couple hours to as long as a few years.

Whenever parents gave up the rights to any of these children over the years, the Gardners adopted them. "More than likely, if they left [the Gardners'], they would've gone to a group home or some kind of place for special-needs children," Sam says. He and his wife felt it was important to give them a real home.

Older children and children with disabilities are very difficult to place, says James Tucker, a lawyer and associate director of the Alabama Disabilities Advocacy Program. Combine the two, and it's almost impossible to find families willing to take on the challenge.

The process of adoption can lead prospective families through a wide range of emotions.

"Children that come to [the Gardner] home do not get turned out," he adds. "We see an alarming number of cases where kids come into foster homes and are not part of that home. With [the Gardners], there's never a doubt that those children are, and remain, a part of that family."

The work involved in having so large a family is constant. "I've had people come in and say: 'You need nurses,' " Bev says, "but my children aren't sick. They have disabilities, but they're healthy, they're whole."

Everyone Pitches In

The Gardners' six-bedroom, two-story home is surprisingly calm and amazingly clean. All 13 children living at home, ranging in age from 6 to 28, have chores.

Brian, who is 9, has become little Lynden's constant companion. Since she can't walk, he pushes her around in her stroller and entertains her with rub-on tattoos.

Tony, 16, helps care for Johnny, 12, and Destin, 14, changing their

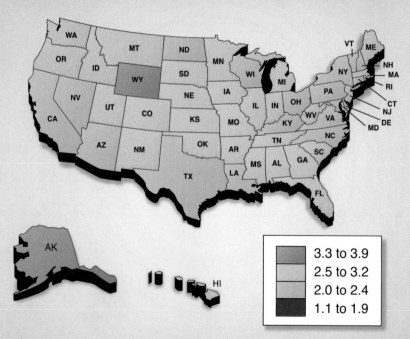

Percent of Children Under 18 of Housholder Who Are Adopted, by State

3.3 to 3.9	
2.5 to 3.2	
2.0 to 2.4	
1.1 to 1.9	

Taken from: Census 2000 Special Reports, "Adopted Children and Stepchildren: 2000," issued October 2003.

diapers and helping to feed them. Tony carries Johnny wherever he needs to go—even though they're almost the same size.

Bev home-schools eight of the children. "They weren't getting what they needed and were getting left behind," she explains. "I know what my kids need. I know how slow they go. We can make things the way they can do the best, and they've done well."

She had doubts about home-schooling in the beginning. "I never thought I could do it. But it's actually been easier. Sending them to public school was harder. This is a good fit for us."

Support from Many Sources

Supporting such a large family is challenging—especially with healthcare costs and the special medical equipment some of the children require. Sam has worked as a shoe salesman at a local department store for 30 years.

The family receives subsidies from the state for the most severely challenged kids, and the community helps.

A local company has bought the children's Christmas presents since 2001. A church group renovated the family's kitchen and dining room.

"A lot of people [who help] say: 'We do this because we can't do what you're doing, so we want to give back in some way,'" Bev says.

"Having one [child] with a disability is a lot of work," says Rod White, director of a baseball league for special-needs children and adults—where the Gardner family has its own team.

"Having a family of children with disabilities is something I can't comprehend," he adds. "And look at [Bev]. She always has a smile on her face. Just the fact that she would take all these kids in, kids that nobody else wanted, and make them her own, to me just says it all."

"I've always pulled for the underdog," Sam says. "We take in kids that would've had a bad family life, and we can see to it that they don't, and that they have a happy family. Family is everything."

EVALUATING THE AUTHOR'S ARGUMENTS:

In this viewpoint, Stetson suggests that the public generally looks favorably upon adoption. What are some reasons why someone might look unfavorably upon adoption?

Adoption Is a Social Ill

Jess DelBalzo and Bryony Lake

"Reproductive exploitation is used as a tool of the billion-dollar adoption industry."

Jess DelBalzo and Bryony Lake argue that reproductive exploitation of women is a tool used in the process of adoption. The authors create analogies with other forms of sexual exploitation in order to support their view that adoption, like other forms of exploitation, ought to be reformed to eliminate the exploitation. DelBalzo is a writer and one of the founding members of Adoption: Legalized Lies, an initiative supporting family preservation. Lake is a member of the First Mothers Action Group and Origins Canada: Supporting People Separated by Adoption.

AS YOU READ, CONSIDER THE FOLLOWING QUESTIONS:
1. What examples do the authors give of "coercive tactics" that they claim are used by adoption workers to get pregnant women to give up their babies?
2. DelBalzo and Lake draw two analogies between adoption and what kind of sexual exploitation?
3. What suggestions do the authors make for eliminating reproductive exploitation through adoption?

In *The Handmaid's Tale*, Margaret Atwood depicted a futuristic society in which fertile young women were held captive and used to bear children for sterile, upper-class wives. The scenario sounds extreme, but sadly, it is not as fictional as one might hope. Vulnerable young women fall victim to reproductive exploitation every day, even in our industrialized North American world.

Exploitation commonly occurs when a powerless group of individuals possesses something that other, more powerful individuals covet. It is nearly unavoidable in a capitalist society, where financial success is often achieved at the expense of innocent men, women, and children.

The exploitation of women, specifically, is not a foreign concept to most of us. For decades, human rights activists have rallied against deplorable working conditions, child prostitution, sexual slavery, and other devastating practices that abuse disadvantaged members of society. Why, then, has reproductive exploitation been ignored?

Reproductive Exploitation

In its most common form, reproductive exploitation is used as a tool of the billion-dollar adoption industry. Well-protected by donations from satisfied adopters, large payments from would-be adopters, and of course the religious and fundamentalist organizations that promote the industry, few people have the opportunity to understand adoption for the business it is.

Advertised as an alternative for infertile couples who desperately want to be "parents," demand for children (and mothers to birth them) is high. Finding pregnant women who are eager to hand their newborn babies over to strangers is next to impossible, and so adoption workers have taken to using coercive tactics against young, poor, and otherwise vulnerable expectant mothers. These mothers-to-be are told that they are selfish if they express the natural desire to keep their children, told that they will quickly get on with their lives and bear other children when they are older/wealthier/married, told that there is no other option available to them. They are not informed of the devastating effect adoption often has on children, nor are they told of the damage adoption will likely inflict on their own psyches. Adoption workers do not care about the well-being of mothers or children, though they may put on a good act to convince expectant parents that their motives are pure. They care about profits, about the image their business is presenting to powerful, potential customers. And there you have it: reproductive exploitation.

Analogies to Adoption

Consider how easily the following quotes about sexual exploitation can be altered to reflect the tactics of the adoption industry:

From [the Community Against Sexual Exploitation of Youth (CASEY)]:

> "Have you ever heard a child say, 'When I grow up, I want to be a prostitute?' For children and youth, working the streets is not a choice. Their lack of life experience and naivety about where the road to the street leads precludes their ability to make a conscious, informed choice."

Now, slightly re-worded:

> "Have you ever heard a little girl say, 'When I grow up, I want to be a birthmother?' For children and youth, surrendering a baby to adoption is not a choice. Their lack of life experience and naivety about the pregnancy/motherhood continuum precludes their ability to make a conscious, informed choice."

Oh darling - let's go upstairs and try for a baby... | Here's one in the States...2000 dollars

Cartoon by Nigel Sutherland. www.CartooonStock.com.

And from [British Columbia's Ministry of Children and Family Development]:

"A sexually exploited youth is someone who is under the age of 18, who has been manipulated or forced into prostitution through perceived affection and belonging, and in return receives drugs, narcotics, money, food and/or shelter."

With a bit of re-wording:

"A reproductively-exploited youth is someone who is under the age of 18, who has been manipulated or forced into surrendering her baby through perceived affection, approval, and promises that the well-being of her baby depends on the baby being turned over to unrelated strangers at birth; and in return receives coverage of medical expenses, shelter, and promises that she can return to pre-pregnant life and will 'get over it.'"

> **FAST FACT**
>
> According to the 2002 National Survey of Family Growth, 2.7 percent of women aged thirty-five to thirty-nine were seeking to adopt.

Of course, reproductive exploitation is not limited to women under the age of 18. Older women are equally at risk, especially when they are poor, unmarried and/or emotionally vulnerable. Just as older women can be sexually exploited, they too can be taken advantage of for their fertility.

Ending Reproductive Exploitation

Though reproductive exploitation has yet to be acknowledged in mainstream society, its existence cannot be denied. Millions of women have been exploited for their fertility in the past 50 years, and millions more will fall prey to such exploitation if measures are not taken to protect them.

As a society, we cannot ethically work to prevent sexual exploitation while allowing women to be exploited by another, equally violent industry. Fertile women who do not wish to become pregnant must be granted access to accurate information about sexual issues, pregnancy, and birth control, as well as access to contraceptives. Women who become pregnant

Many women in third world countries are victims of reproductive exploitation. This woman from a poverty-stricken Cambodian village was asked to sell her two-month old twins to a family overseas.

either by choice or by chance must be treated with respect regardless of their age, financial situation, or marital status. They must be informed of their rights and given access to all available resources to help them raise their children. They must be armed with information about any decision they make. And above all, they must not be coerced, lied to, or shamed into believing that adoption is their only option. These protections against reproductive exploitation must be made into law.

Now-powerless fertile women will be empowered. Their children will be treated as human beings, rather than as "product" to be sold. The only loser will be the adoption industry—and when you look at it that way, everyone wins.

**EVALUATING THE AUTHORS'
ARGUMENTS:**

In this viewpoint Jess DelBalzo and Bryony Lake claim reproductive exploitation has been used because it is so difficult to get pregnant women willingly to give their babies to strangers. What might constitute an uncoerced reason for a woman to be willing to have her baby adopted by someone else?

Adoption Can Help End Abortion

Nathan Tabor

"Adoption truly is the alternative to abortion."

In the following viewpoint Nathan Tabor argues that Americans who are against abortion ought to consider adoption. Tabor believes that there are two issues that explain why many Americans do not consider adoption. In addition Tabor believes that pregnant women currently find abortion a much simpler process. Arguing that the process needs to be made easier for both adoptive parents and pregnant women, Tabor concludes that more adoptions would mean fewer abortions. Tabor is a conservative political activist based in North Carolina and founder of the Web site The Conservative Voice.

AS YOU READ, CONSIDER THE FOLLOWING QUESTIONS:
  1. How has the antiabortion movement made progress in Washington, D.C., according to the author's quote from President George W. Bush?
  2. On what issue does Tabor agree with abortion-rights activists?
  3. According to the author, what two issues need to be changed in order to make adoption as easy to choose as abortion?

rowds of pro-life Americans filled the streets of Washington, D.C. this week [January 2005] to protest the 32 years of bloody infanticide that have followed the immoral *Roe v. Wade* decision of 1973. March for Life organizers estimated that more than 250,000 hardy souls braved the bitter cold to stand in defense of innocent unborn children.

Fighting Abortion

A variety of speakers urged the assembled activists to stay the course, promising victory ahead. With several appointments to the Supreme Court in the offing, the prospect for reversing the *Roe* decision seems more real than it has in recent years.

President George W. Bush encouraged the marchers by telephone from Camp David. "We're making progress in Washington," Bush insisted, on issues like partial birth abortion, legal protection for infants that survive an attempted abortion, the right of doctors and nurses to refuse to perform abortions on the grounds of conscience, and criminal prosecution for those who harm or kill a fetus while committing a crime against the mother. All positive developments.

"We are working to promote a culture of life, to promote compassion for women and their unborn babies," the President declared. But Bush also issued a solemn challenge to the crowd.

"I encourage you to take heart from our achievements, because a true culture of life cannot be sustained solely by changing laws. We need, most of all, to change hearts," Bush declared.

FAST FACT

According to the Child Welfare Information Gateway, over one-third of Americans have considered adopting, whereas no more than 2 percent of Americans have actually adopted.

Adoption as Part of the Solution

There are many in America who preach against abortion—which I completely agree with. But there are very few who preach for the adoption of those innocent children "rescued" from abortion. Frankly, this reeks of hypocrisy. Abortion-rights activists are always challenging

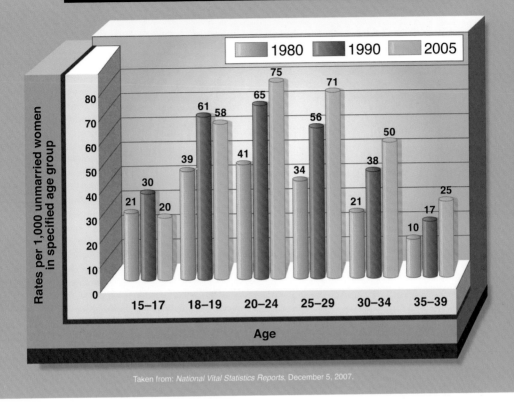

Birth Rates for Unmarried Women by Age: United States, 1980, 1990, and 2005

Legend: 1980, 1990, 2005

Rates per 1,000 unmarried women in specified age group

Age	1980	1990	2005
15–17	21	30	20
18–19	39	61	58
20–24	41	65	75
25–29	34	56	71
30–34	21	38	50
35–39	10	17	25

Taken from: *National Vital Statistics Reports*, December 5, 2007.

pro-life Christians about whether or not they have adopted. I believe this is quite fair. Remember the familiar phrase, "Put your money where your mouth is"?

We say we reverence human life, and we repudiate the heartless mother who would slay the innocent child within her womb. But do we care enough to take that unwanted child into our own home and give it the love and nurturing that it needs to grow up to adulthood? We need to show our love not only in word but also in deed.

President Bush spoke of "The America of our dreams, where every child is welcomed in life, and protected by law." Yes, we want those babies protected by law . . . but are we willing to make personal sacrifices to welcome them into life?

Adoption truly is the alternative to abortion. Showing birth mothers that their little ones will have a safe and loving home will go a long way toward changing their hearts.

Pro-life demonstrators march alongside abortion advocates in Washington, D.C. on the thirty-second anniversary of the Roe v. Wade *decision. Some feel that promoting adoption could lead to fewer abortions.*

Making Adoption More Popular

It is a fact that an abortion is fairly simple to attain as well as inexpensive, while adoption is quite a tedious and costly process. Many parents are forced to go overseas to adopt because of the regulations and costs. Most adoptions in America take place only because of a couple's infertility. I understand we must be careful about who adopts and their intentions. Still, we need to streamline the process and lower the cost of adoptions in the USA.

On a personal note, my parents were foster parents, so I grew up with other children sitting around the table with my two natural brothers and me. I saw firsthand how much good a loving family can do in the life of a child who has no one else.

Last week, my wife Jordan gave birth to our first child, a precious little baby girl. We have talked and both agree that we would like to adopt a child one day. What about you?

According to their 2003–04 Annual Report, Planned Parenthood's clinics aborted 138 children for every one time they referred their clients to an outside agency for adoption. But Crisis Pregnancy Centers are the pro-life alternative to Planned Parenthood clinics. They offer a haven of hope and unconditional love for both the unwed mother and her unborn child. I serve on the board of the Hope Crisis Pregnancy Center in King, NC.

We need to support these centers with both our time and our money.

EVALUATING THE AUTHOR'S ARGUMENTS:

In this viewpoint Nathan Tabor claims that getting more families to adopt can help reduce the number of abortions. What assumption is Tabor making about women who choose abortion in order to reach this conclusion?

Adoption Cannot End Abortion

David Nova

"Good adoption law won't end abortion."

In the following viewpoint David Nova argues that although adoption is often talked about as if it were an alternative to abortion, it rarely is. Nova does not believe that promoting adoption is the route to ending abortion. Nova points to reasons that go beyond a lack of information about adoption or availability of adoptive parents to explain why women with unwanted pregnancies are so reluctant to consider adoption. Nova is president and CEO of Planned Parenthood of the Blue Ridge in Virginia.

AS YOU READ, CONSIDER THE FOLLOWING QUESTIONS:

1. According to the author, what three ways of reducing unwanted pregnancy would be far more effective in helping to end abortion than good adoption law?
2. What do women with unwanted pregnancies believe about adoption, according to Nova?
3. In what ways does the author claim pregnant women who choose adoption feel stigmatized by society?

Talking about adoption on the campaign trail rarely alienates voters. It's the rhetorical equivalent of kissing babies. Yet, Laura Effel ("An unrealistic answer to abortion," Oct. 17 [2004]) criticized President Bush for his adoption comment during the second presidential debate. She accused him of raising an "old misconception: That if we could only encourage mothers with unwanted pregnancies to give up their children for adoption, we could go a long way toward preventing abortion."

The president's mention of adoption came late in that debate: "I think it is a worthy goal in America to have every child protected by law and welcomed in life. I also think we ought to continue to have good adoption law as an alternative to abortion." Of course, neither candidate suggested we discontinue having good adoption law. Rather than champion adoption, the president used his comment to deftly sidestep the divisive issue of abortion. Baby kissed. Next question.

When faced with an unwanted pregnancy, many women consider both abortion and adoption. Some feel that the adoption option does not reduce the chances that a woman will choose abortion.

Adoption Not a Real Alternative

Good adoption law won't end abortion. Reducing unwanted pregnancy through increased access to contraception, medically accurate sexuality education and more open communication within families would be far more efficacious. Yet, Americans' misconceptions of adoption certainly compound the problem. In America, adoption is the favorite choice that nobody wants to take.

At Planned Parenthood's Roanoke Center—the only medical facility in the nation with on-site adoption, abortion and prenatal care—the choice of adoption is relatively rare. We perform more than 500 abortions and close to 3,000 prenatal visits annually. Though several dozen patients may seriously consider adoption, very few end up placing their child in the loving home of an adopting family.

Our patient numbers are somewhat skewed. (Our opponents only market our abortion services in the community.) Yet our patient trends mimic those at the national level.

Adoption is the least understood and least attractive pregnancy option for our pregnant patients. In their minds, adoption involves nine months of pregnancy followed by a difficult labor. When the baby is born, the umbilical cord is cut and the child is whisked away, only to appear on the doorstep 18 years later wanting to know why he or she was abandoned.

> **FAST FACT**
>
> The number of abortions performed in the United States dropped to 1.2 million in 2005—the lowest level since 1976.

Modern adoption, often referred to as "open adoption," harbors little resemblance to these nightmarish impressions. With open adoption, the birth mother has far more control. She decides who will adopt the child and what ongoing (though limited) relationship she will have with both the child and the adopting family. With greater latitude in deciding the outcome of her life and the life of her baby, adoption could be a far more attractive option for pregnant women—if more of them knew about it.

President Bush, and for that matter Sen. John Kerry, could have taken 30 seconds during the debate to educate on open adoption. Not

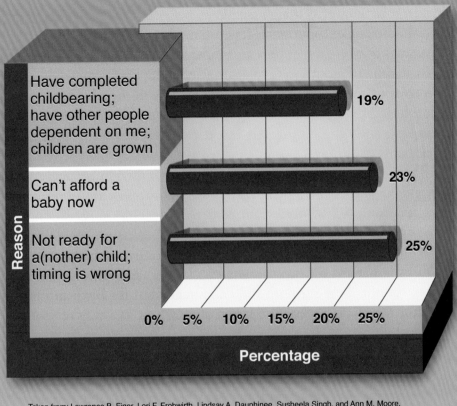

Top Three Most Important Reasons Given for Abortion, 2004

Have completed childbearing; have other people dependent on me; children are grown — 19%

Can't afford a baby now — 23%

Not ready for a(nother) child; timing is wrong — 25%

Reason

Percentage

Taken from: Lawrence B. Finer, Lori F. Frohwirth, Lindsay A. Dauphinee, Susheela Singh, and Ann M. Moore, "Reasons U.S. Women Have Abortions: Quantitative and Qualitative Perspectives," *Perspectives on Sexual and Reproductive Health*, 2005, p. 114.

only would this have served the public good, it would have rightfully scored political points with voters.

The Stigma of Adoption

The candidates could also have used their many public appearances to improve America's ambivalent attitude toward birth mothers. Adopting a child is considered noble and compassionate. However, Americans are often harsh critics of birth mothers who, in the words of Effel and so many others, "give up their children." That phrase connotes abandonment and underlies the shame some birth mothers are made to feel by family, acquaintances and the general public.

Unlike abortion, there is no hiding pregnancy for a woman choosing adoption. A pregnant physique invites questions from strangers and acquaintances. Have you picked out a name? Decorated the nursery? Held a baby shower? Though seemingly benign, such daily queries can be awkward and uncomfortable for birth mothers. They serve as constant reminders to women that they are bucking society's expectations.

At Planned Parenthood, we learned this the hard way when prospective birth mothers did not want to meet with the adoption counselor during their prenatal visits. They feared other pregnant women who were choosing motherhood would realize they were "giving up their baby."

The adoption counselors from the Children's Home Society of Virginia now meet with prospective birth mothers in the administrative and education wings of our centers in order to keep the choice of adoption confidential.

Women would more likely choose adoption were they not made to feel stigmatized for their pregnancy choice. The president, and all of us, should show support and encouragement for birth mothers, but not merely as a means to lessen abortion or as a way of scoring political points.

Supporting birth mothers should reflect a larger aspiration in which every woman has the freedom to thoughtfully consider the personal choice that is best for her and her family. Providing such leadership would benefit the country and the American people. It would also make kissing babies on the campaign trail look far less like an empty political gesture.

EVALUATING THE AUTHORS' ARGUMENTS:

In this viewpoint David Nova argues that promoting adoption is not a good way to end abortion. What changes to the adoption process and society's views might Nathan Tabor suggest could make adoption a viable alternative to abortion, resulting in a decrease in abortion?

Adoption Can Help Other Countries

Talia Carner

"The abandoned infants adopted by foreigners are otherwise doomed."

In the following viewpoint Talia Carner argues that American adoption of Chinese orphans helps to uphold the basic human right to live. Carner counts China's one-child policy, the traditional favoring of boy children, and a disinterest in human rights among the reasons for the large number of orphans, primarily girls, in need of adoptive parents. Carner calls for further inquiry into China's claim regarding the lack of supply of available babies. Carner is author of the novel *China Doll* and an activist against infanticide in China.

AS YOU READ, CONSIDER THE FOLLOWING QUESTIONS:
1. According to Carner, what is China's national boy-to-girl ratio compared to the worldwide ratio?
2. What three internal problems does the author cite as possible reasons for China's newly restrictive adoption policy?
3. What will happen as a result of China's policy that restricts the qualified pool of American adoptive parents, according to Carner?

China's recent announcement of tighter guidelines for foreign adoption, together with a claim that the supply of available babies could not meet growing demand, surprised many.

How could there be a shortage when even the government-controlled Chinese press reports that thousands of babies are abandoned or killed shortly after birth, while many others are forcibly aborted?

Chinese Girls

Looking at the 2005 Unicef annual birth report and the Chinese government 2006 report of the country's boys-to-girls ratio, one would expect to find 1.7 million more girls than appear.

The gap in the boy-to-girl ratio has been growing, particularly in regions where the one-child policy collides with traditional favoring of boys, to a national average ratio of 122-to-100, and in some regions to a ratio of 140-to-100—not to mention places like Xicun village in southern Guangxi province where there are five boys to every girl. The average worldwide ratio is 105-to-100.

Of the 1.7 million "missing" girls, activists and Western charity workers believe, hundreds of thousands are due to sex-selection abortions, many are unregistered, living "illegally" with their or adoptive

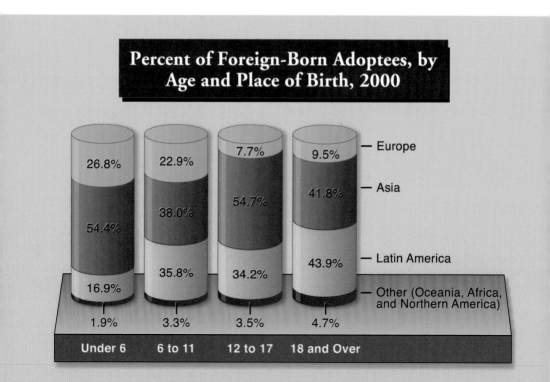

Percent of Foreign-Born Adoptees, by Age and Place of Birth, 2000

Under 6: Europe 26.8%, Asia 54.4%, Latin America 16.9%, Other (Oceania, Africa, and Northern America) 1.9%

6 to 11: Europe 22.9%, Asia 38.0%, Latin America 35.8%, Other (Oceania, Africa, and Northern America) 3.3%

12 to 17: Europe 7.7%, Asia 54.7%, Latin America 34.2%, Other (Oceania, Africa, and Northern America) 3.5%

18 and Over: Europe 9.5%, Asia 41.8%, Latin America 43.9%, Other (Oceania, Africa, and Northern America) 4.7%

Taken from: U.S. Census Bureau, Census 2000 special tabulations.

families, and hundreds of thousands are abandoned. Presum: found are sent to orphanages, although the 2005 China reports between 200,000 and 300,000 abandoned children local jurisdictions disclaim responsibility and who there~~~~ ~~~~ reach orphanages.

China's Adoption Policy

In 1995, before blocking information on its orphanages, China reported 40,000 such institutions. While hundreds have since been either disbanded or improved thanks to Western charities, estimates are that over 39,000 orphanages still operate. As may be gleaned from the government's published miniscule budgets, "orphans," or more accurately, abandoned infants, most likely are living in inhuman conditions or suffering fatal neglect.

So what gives? The fewer than 10,000 female infants adopted by foreigners last year represent a drop of water in the sea of unwanted

FAST FACT

According to the U.S. Census in 2000, there are more adopted girls in U.S. families than adopted boys.

babies. Are the Chinese so concerned about their babies' future that they want to ensure they don't fall into the arms of fat or ugly parents— whom the new criteria consider inappropriate—or those who, after shelling out close to $30,000 for the adoption process, might be unable to pay college tuition?

Possible reasons for China's stance lie with its internal problems.

Corruption is one reason. A new opportunity for corruption has appeared this past decade with the flow of over $100 million directly into the hands of orphanage directors. According to one report, only 10% of the between $3,000 and $5,000 Western adoptive parents leave behind ever reaches the children of the orphanages.

Since American cash "donations" are a lot of money in a country where average monthly income is about $25, the incentive to sell more babies is great. Directors of orphanages designated for foreign adoptions therefore have been tempted to purchase babies for, say, $150, and the operators they deal with often buy babies for as low as $8. Or, as has been reported, they just kidnap them.

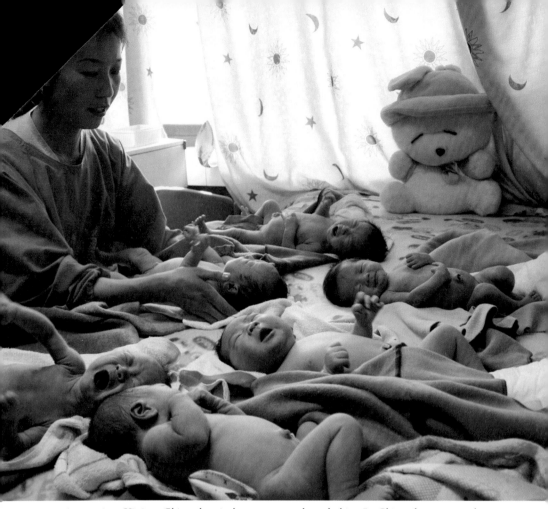

A nurse in a Xining, China, hospital massages newborn babies. In China, boys outnumber girls by a ratio of 122 to 100 due to the effects of the government's One Child Policy.

Another reason is a totalitarian government's need for control. An editor at the *Epoch Times* newspaper, Janet Xiong, explains that whenever there is a surge in activity of any kind, the Chinese government seeks to maintain control. "The government must make sure everyone knows who's in charge," she says. "Tightening the rules—for adoption or anything that shows a surge—is the end goal of a Communist regime."

"Saving face" is yet another reason. China is interested in its international image, and from its perspective, the availability of so many of its infants doesn't look good. So it denies their existence, and hence, the "shortage". Furthermore, according to New York–based human-rights activist, Dr. Wenyi Wang, the Chinese government cannot accept that life in a democratic society may be more advantageous for Chinese children.

Policy Denies Human Rights

What about humane considerations? The abandoned infants adopted by foreigners are otherwise doomed. And the new stringent adoption rules that limit the qualified pool of adoptive parents by age, weight, income, health, sexual orientation, and marital status deny disabled or older Chinese children the medical care and life in a family they desperately need.

But such "humane considerations never come into play," Dr. Wang says. "Nothing matters. China has never catered to individuals' needs, nor shown regard for human suffering."

So why are we surprised that babies are not made available?

Western attention has focused on a myriad of China's human rights abuses. But gendercide is not covered in Human Rights Watch's report released this month, is given five words in the 2005 U.S. State Department report, gets a passing nod in the World Health Organization report, and is not even mentioned by the 2006 U.S. Congressional-Executive Commission on China, mandated in 2000 with monitoring human rights in China.

Perhaps if we raise our collective indignation about this most basic human right—the right to live—we will send a clear message to China. Let's ask tough questions and, with the upcoming 2008 Olympics in Beijing, send journalists to poke around. Ms. Xiong believes that adoption rules may relax as suddenly as they were imposed. Or maybe not.

EVALUATING THE AUTHOR'S ARGUMENTS:

In this viewpoint Talia Carner claims that the international adoption of (mainly female) orphans helps to relieve the human rights abuses in China. Given her claims about the possible corruption of orphanage directors and the operators they deal with, should adoption of Chinese orphans continue? Why or why not?

Adoption Cannot Help Other Countries

Stan Chu Ilo

"These interventionist approaches address symptoms while ignoring root causes."

In the following viewpoint Stan Chu Ilo argues that the adoption of African orphans by Europeans and North Americans is not a sustainable solution. Ilo claims that the large number of orphans in Africa is symptomatic of deeper problems. The solution to the orphan problem involves examining deeper issues and helping African nations to develop sustainable solutions that do not depend on Western solutions such as adoption. Ilo is a Catholic priest of the Igbo tribe in Eastern Nigeria and a doctoral student on the faculty of theology at St. Michael's University in the University of Toronto, Canada.

AS YOU READ, CONSIDER THE FOLLOWING QUESTIONS:
1. According to the author, Africa has how many orphans?
2. Ilo claims that the absence of what frameworks in Africa gives rise to crises such as the current orphan crisis?
3. In order to address the orphan problem, the author believes that questions need to be posed about what three causes of the parents' early deaths?

Stan Chu Ilo, "Madonna's Adoption of David Raises Bigger Questions About Africa," *National Catholic Reporter,* vol. 43, November 17, 2006, p. 18. Copyright © 2006 The National Catholic Reporter Publishing Company, 115 E. Armour Blvd., Kansas City, MO 64111. All rights reserved. Reproduced by permission of the author.

The controversy over the adoption of a 1-year-old Malawian orphan, David, by Madonna raises a number of important questions about adoptions of African orphans to Europe and North America.

My concern here is not to debate the morality or legality of this adoption, even though these have implications for Baby David's future happiness, fundamental rights, stability and cultural integration. The court in Malawi has allowed conditional 18-month interim adoption pending the resolution of legal issues raised by a coalition of 67 human rights groups in Malawi.

Orphans in Africa

My concern is whether adoption of African orphans to Western countries offers any meaningful answer to the challenges that high numbers of orphans pose to African societies: What do we do about the millions of orphans whose numbers are growing by the day as poverty, HIV/AIDS and civil unrest continue to take their heavy toll on parents who are often cut down in the prime of life?

Africa is home to over 48 million orphans. According to UNICEF, 12 percent of children living in Africa are orphans and the number is expected to rise to 20 percent in about five years. Baby David was one of 900,000 orphans living in Malawi. There are about 12 million African orphans who have lost a parent to AIDS. The rest of the African orphans are those who have lost either or both parents through wars and civil unrest, diseases like malaria and typhoid fever, and high rates of maternal mortality. What is their fate? The answer cannot be found in film stars, or even in outside relief aid. Something more fundamental is required.

Orphans Symptom of a Larger Problem

The challenge of constructing coherent, balanced and sustainable development practices for Africa cannot be met by random involvement by Westerners, whether they are celebrities, high-profile politicians or ordinary people. Such approaches are attempts to respond to crises that result from the failure by Africans and the international community to evolve long-term development policy and programs. These interventionist approaches address symptoms while ignoring root causes.

Pop singer Madonna's adoption of David, a Malawian orphan, has raised issues about the welfare of African children orphaned when their parents die of AIDS.

Sustainable development in Africa can only come about through a conscious approach on the part of Africans and Western governments and agencies to develop and promote basic institutional frameworks with regard to agriculture, education, health, infrastructural development and governance in Africa. The absence of these frameworks gives rise to this revolving chain of crises and dependency that have beleaguered African nations since their independence more than four decades ago.

There is an urgent need for a crisis response approach to the heart-wrenching conditions in some parts of Africa now, particularly in Darfur, Northern Uganda, Sierra Leone, Liberia, Congo-Kinshasa, Somalia, Malawi, and the African Sahel region. In these areas, there is grave need for some form of interventionist approach with regard to diseases, rehabilitation of refugees, droughts and starvation, and the restoration of law and order.

But a new approach is urgently needed to kick-start genuine development, both in these areas and elsewhere.

Questions to Ask to Solve the Problem

According to the U.N. Millennium Development Goals' report, Africa is the only continent where the standard of living has been falling progressively during the last four decades. Life was actually better in Africa in 1966 than it is right now. Why have the various donor initiatives in Africa not helped in laying a solid foundation for sustainable development? When will the continent stand on its feet? What contributions should churches, donor agencies and Western governments make to help stimulate sustained growth and development?

FAST FACT

According to UNICEF, at the close of 2003, of the forty sub-Saharan countries with a generalized HIV epidemic, only six had a national policy on orphans and other vulnerable children.

Africa should become the centerpiece of global action targeted at building up its institutions at the grass-roots level. In this regard, both Africans and Westerners have great responsibility. Westerners who raise all the funds or whose governments channel a part of their taxes to development initiatives in Africa should begin to hold their governments, donor agencies and churches to account on how they are realizing the objectives they set out to achieve in Africa.

What are the institutional frameworks and structural conditioning of African societies that have made them susceptible to political, economic

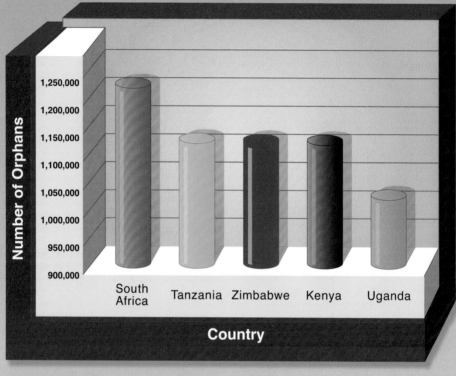

Countries in Africa with 1 Million or More Orphans Due to AIDS

Number of Orphans

- 1,250,000
- 1,200,000
- 1,150,000
- 1,100,000
- 1,050,000
- 1,000,000
- 950,000
- 900,000

South Africa   Tanzania   Zimbabwe   Kenya   Uganda

Country

Taken from: Avert.org, 2005.

and social crises? Why are the governments of Africa unworkable and ineffective in addressing the needs of their people? Why are African countries more susceptible to diseases and natural disasters? Is there a real basis for nationhood in African countries or are these countries mockeries of true nationhood with lack of freedoms that translates into a refurbished servitude in the hands of corrupt politicians and ethnic champions?

Each challenge or crisis reveals a deeper problem to be addressed. For instance, if one were to truly address the orphan problem, one would ask about the poverty, civil wars and diseases that lead to parents' early deaths.

Orphan Problem Not Solved by Adoption

Development aid should be proactive, supporting the mechanization of agriculture and a burgeoning clothing industry, for example, rather than just sending food and used tennis-shoes. Training Africans to become doctors, engineers and pharmacists, and building well-equipped clinics should be stressed over sending doctors with drugs to work for one or two months.

The mass media are filled with advertisements showing the pain and misery in Africa and asking people to make donations. They give a false picture of the African condition, framing it in a mold that elicits sympathy and donations while hiding the other face waiting to be born. There is no integrated approach, no sensitivity to the cultural, political and economic realities of the African world, no emphasis on dynamic and inherent possibilities, and no inclusion of the African peoples at the grass-roots level in the articulation of these plans.

Developing the capacity of Africans to apply themselves to their cultural world, to apply their skills to their environment with all that it contains in terms of material resources, should be a major priority of Western relief agencies.

What caused the death of Baby David's mother? What should be done to prevent African mothers from the high mortality rate associated with childbirth and the high incidence of HIV/AIDS infection? Why is Baby David's father so helpless that he is gladly giving away his son for adoption in a society where male children are valued as the guarantee for one's ancestral life? Why is Baby David's grandmother so poor that she could not support her grandson?

Answering these questions is more important and more fundamental than adopting an African orphan.

EVALUATING THE AUTHOR'S ARGUMENTS:

In this viewpoint Stan Chu Ilo argues that adoption of African orphans is not a solution. With that in mind, what do you think he would say to an American family considering adoption of an African orphan at the present time? Do you think Ilo's response would be the same as or different from Talia Carner's response to the family?

Chapter 2

What Types of Adoption Should Be Encouraged?

Adoption by homosexual couples continues to be a controversial issue.

There Are Good Reasons to Discourage Adoption by Homosexual Couples

Father Thomas D. Williams

"The adoption issue has often been mistakenly identified as a question of gay rights."

In the following viewpoint Father Thomas D. Williams argues that Catholic Charities are justified in denying adoption to homosexuals. Williams claims that no one has a right to adopt a child, and agencies making decisions about parents discriminate in a variety of ways. Williams believes that requiring a mother and a father for children who are to be adopted is a reasonable requirement that has the best interest of the child in mind. Williams is dean of the theology school at Rome's Regina Apostolorum University and Vatican Analyst for NBC News and MSNBC.

Father Thomas D. Williams, "Let Catholic Charities Be Catholic," *National Review Online,* March 21, 2006. Reproduced by permission.

AS YOU READ, CONSIDER THE FOLLOWING QUESTIONS:
1. What example of justified discrimination of prospective parents does Williams use in order to make the case that calling certain practices of adoption agencies discriminatory is not an argument against such practices?
2. What two examples of negative effects on children does the author cite in order to support the conclusion that parenting by both a mother and a father is preferable?
3. What does Williams think is flawed about the consideration of the income of prospective parents, without consideration of gender?

Much fuss is being made over Boston's Catholic Charities' refusal to place children with same-sex couples in its adoption services. The political agenda behind the garment-rending and name-calling should have more than Catholics up in arms.

Let me start by saying that I wouldn't expect everyone to agree with the criteria employed by Catholic Charities in its selection process. After all, the Church attempts to find a home that provides not only material comfort, but also a morally and spiritually sound environment according to its own standards and perspective. A living arrangement that the Church considers to be objectively sinful doesn't qualify as being in children's best interests. But no one is required to make use of the Catholic agency, and plenty of other options exist for those who disagree.

Justified Discrimination

What I would strenuously resist is an attempt to make religiously inspired or private agencies conform to a one-size-fits-all, state-imposed model of parental selection. The Christian Church has been looking after widows, orphans, and the destitute since long before the U.S. federal government came into existence. Why should a secular model trump other legitimate standards for adoption? Isn't that, after all, why a variety of adoption agencies came into existence—to provide parents with options that correspond to their values and concerns? In what way does a *de facto* secular monopoly serve the common good better than a range of adoption alternatives?

Let's cut through the rhetoric of "discrimination" that only clouds the issue. The simple fact is that *all* adoption agencies discriminate—that is the purpose of the evaluation of prospective parents. Candidates must run a gruelling gauntlet of tests, interviews, and questionnaires covering everything from their financial situation to their personal histories, education and criminal record. The commonwealth of Massachusetts applies any number of litmus tests to weed out unsuitable candidates. Let's just take the example of financial discrimination. The poor may not adopt. In order to adopt, couples must not only demonstrate economic solvency, but wealth. I personally know of several loving, married, middle-class couples that have been denied adoption simply because their bank account wasn't big enough. The question then becomes, not whether agencies should discriminate, but rather, on what grounds they should discriminate.

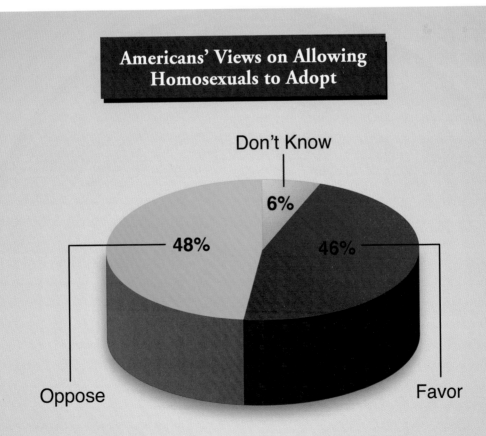

Americans' Views on Allowing Homosexuals to Adopt

Don't Know

6%

48%

46%

Oppose

Favor

Taken from: Pew Research Center for the People and the Press, March 8–12, 2006.

The Importance of a Mother and Father

Catholic Charities believes that same-sex caregivers do not provide an atmosphere that is conducive to the well-rounded rearing of children. Despite all the talk of generic "parenting," mothers and fathers are not androgynous, interchangeable "parental units." A mother is not expendable and cannot be replaced by a second father. When she is missing, something essential is lost. To deliberately deprive a child of a mother or a father is to do violence to that child. Moreover, not only are both parents necessary for the unique contribution each provides, they also furnish an example of interaction between the sexes themselves.

Some feel that it is not in the best interest of children to be raised by same-sex couples.

There is not enough sound statistical evidence about children raised by single-sex caregivers to determine definitively what long-term effects this arrangement will have. Still, what evidence does exist gives serious cause for concern. Most studies suggest that mothers' and fathers' complementary input aids in a child's psycho-sexual development, and studies show that children raised by single-sex caregivers have a much higher rate of gender dissatisfaction.

FAST FACT

Approximately 2 million gay, lesbian, or bisexual people in America are interested in adopting.

Again, none of it (and there's more) is conclusive, but it does illustrate the reasonableness of the position taken by Catholic Charities. Adoption agencies exist in order to help children, not to subject them to experiments in progressive social engineering whose long-term effects are not certain. Where serious doubt exists, prudence would dictate following the less risky path.

Meeting the Needs of Children

Some have countered that entrusting children to gay couples, while perhaps not the best option, beats the alternatives. There simply are not enough available married couples willing to adopt, and gays fill the gap. Yet this logic is based on two false premises. First, there are long lines of married couples waiting to adopt a child, many of whom spend years navigating the labyrinthine adoption process. Most often, what are lacking are not adoptive parents, but children to adopt. The process can become so frustrating and drawn out that many opt for other alternatives, like adopting a child from a foreign country. Second, where gay adoption is permitted, no special rules apply granting preference to married couples, and children are placed indiscriminately with homosexual couples and heterosexuals. Once again, the determining factor often becomes income, as if a plasma television, MP3 player, and Game Boy were more important for a child than a mother and father.

Finally, the adoption issue has often been mistakenly identified as a question of gay rights. Yet children are not a commodity that all should "have," and no one has the *right* to adopt. Children do, however, have the right to a mother and a father. Adoption is not about filling an emotional void in adults' lives, but offering a stable home to unfortunate children. When political agendas prevail over the best interests of children, sloppy moral reasoning is sure to follow.

Adoption reform is long overdue, and much bureaucratic dead wood needs to be hewn out of the adoption process. Yet this reform must be carried out in a way that favors the physical, emotional, and spiritual needs of children. If Catholic Charities chooses to raise the bar a little higher, they should be congratulated rather than vilified.

EVALUATING THE AUTHOR'S ARGUMENTS:

In this viewpoint Father Thomas D. Williams argues that it is reasonable for agencies to place adopted children only with heterosexual couples and that there are long lines of married couples waiting to adopt. Using Williams's analysis based on what he argues is good for the child, do you think he would agree that children who are not otherwise being adopted (because of age or disability, for instance) should never be placed with homosexuals? Why or why not?

Viewpoint

2

Adoption by Homosexual Couples Should Not Be Discouraged

"I am grieved by this rejection of love freely offered, selflessly and heroically."

Jo McGowan

In the following viewpoint Jo McGowan argues that adoption by homosexuals should be welcomed. McGowan gives reasons to believe that not only are many gay and lesbian couples just as equipped as many heterosexual couples to parent, she also argues that in one way they may be better equipped to deal with the unique needs of the adopted child. She concludes that couples who are willing to offer love to an adopted child, whether same sex or opposite sex, should be able to adopt. McGowan is a writer and the parent of an adopted child.

AS YOU READ, CONSIDER THE FOLLOWING QUESTIONS:

1. According to McGowan, what unique needs does an adopted child have?

2. Why is the author, as a Catholic, particularly outraged at the decision by Catholic Charities of Boston to deny gay couples the ability to adopt?
3. Why does the author believe that gay couples are better suited to care for the unique needs of adopted children?

I have always been a strong advocate of adoption. It is a family tradition: my parents adopted my sister; my husband and I adopted our youngest, my sister and her husband adopted their little girl; and my brother-in-law and his wife adopted both their children. There was a time when I thought of starting an adoption agency because it seemed the perfect answer to two deep human yearnings: a child needs parents, parents want a child. What could be simpler? In fact few things can be more complicated.

I have stopped advocating, stopped trying to persuade young couples to adopt before having a homemade baby, stopped trying to convince the world that "Each One Take One" is the solution to the problems of abortion and unwanted children.

I still believe fervently in adoption. I still thank God every day for my sister, my daughter, my nieces, and my nephew. I just know now that it isn't necessarily the right thing for everyone to do. I believe couples considering adoption should be far better prepared for the journey they are embarking on, and far clearer about the guaranteed burdens the new baby coming into their family will bear.

FAST FACT

According to a recent study, gay and lesbian parents are raising 4 percent of all adopted children in the United States.

Unique Needs of the Adopted Child

A child who has been abandoned by its mother, no matter how dire the circumstances, no matter how sensible her decision, suffers a loss nothing can make up for. Life contains sorrows that cannot be assuaged, and it is important to be honest in acknowledging this. Too often, in our desire to believe in the healing powers of love, we deny the power of grief.

Couples volunteering to be the parents of such a child need to understand this and to realize the enormity of what they are taking on. When my husband and I adopted our baby daughter, Moy Moy, we were as innocent as babies ourselves. She was twelve weeks premature, but I think our pre-maturity was far more profound. Lucky for us, and for her, some things were given: we were deeply in love, we had already raised two homemade children, and I was a stay-at-home mom.

That stay-at-home bit is crucial. Somebody—man or woman—has to be willing to do it. A baby who has been abandoned needs to be held more often, cuddled more convincingly, and loved in ways that go beyond "quality time." That baby needs unconditional acceptance, and she needs it constantly.

Gay Couples Uniquely Equipped to Adopt

The recent decision by Catholic Charities of Boston—under unwarranted pressure from both the bishops of Massachusetts and from

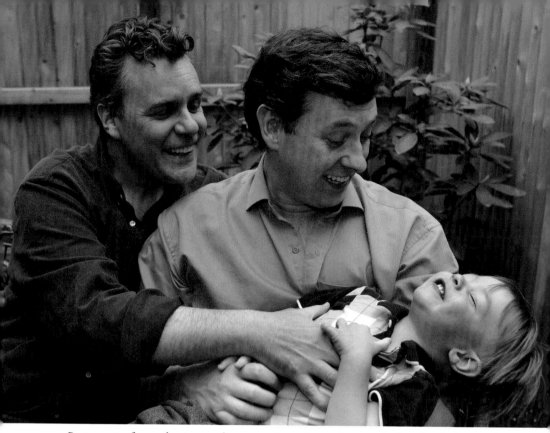

Proponents of gay adoption say homosexual couples are better suited to the challenges of raising children with unconditional acceptance.

the Vatican—to refuse to allow gay couples to adopt children, is an example of wrongheadedness and intransigence that would make the angels weep. It is a disgrace to all that the church stands for, and it is an indictment of all that we believe about the sanctity of life and the gift that every child represents. As a Catholic, I am grieved by this rejection of love freely offered, selflessly and heroically. As the mother of an adopted child, I am amazed at the stupidity of a policy that denies the unique capacity of gay couples to provide what would be adoptive children so desperately need.

Without being sentimental or biased, it is possible to say that certain people, because of their life experiences, are better qualified for certain tasks than others. People with disabilities, for example, and those who work with them, are more likely to be able to accept others as they are, simply because they have more experience doing it. People with disabilities may drool or have difficulty in expressing themselves. They may use sign language rather than words, or read Braille rather than conventional print. Those who are disabled themselves, or who have experience with people with disabilities, tend to be calmer about the variety of life's gifts, knowing it is the same Spirit who provides them.

Similarly, gay couples, having staked everything on love in a world that is often hostile toward them, let alone tolerant, are better suited than most to the challenges of caring for children who need unconditional acceptance. If, having risked being ostracized and rejected by the community they—like anyone else—desire to be a part of, they are still willing to offer their lives and their hearts as a haven for children in the most desperate need of protection and unconditional acceptance, who on earth are we to say they are unworthy?

As a Catholic, I say no to the decision by Boston Catholic Charities to refuse to provide adoption services to gay couples. Love is rare enough in this world of violence and meanness. Can we truly consider rejecting it because it comes from people of the same sex?

EVALUATING THE AUTHORS' ARGUMENTS:

In this viewpoint Jo McGowan claims that gay couples are uniquely situated to meet the needs of adopted children. How do you think the author of the previous viewpoint, Father Thomas D. Williams, would respond to this claim?

Transracial Adoption of African American Children Is Needed

"The number of infertile black couples who can afford to adopt is simply not as large as the number of black babies available."

Dawn Davenport

In the following viewpoint Dawn Davenport claims that there is a lack of adoptive families in America willing to adopt African American children. Davenport reports on the recent trend of foreign families (mainly white) adopting black children from the United States. Davenport claims that the reason for the surplus of African American children is the lack of white American families willing to adopt black children coupled with the lack of available African American adoptive parents. Davenport is a researcher, attorney, adoption expert, and author of *The Complete Book on International Adoption*. Her Web site is www.creatinga family.com.

1. What reason, besides racism, is offered by the author as an explanation of why American families choose to adopt abroad rather than adopt a black American child?
2. According to Davenport, what are the approximate adoption fees for Caucasian babies, biracial babies, and African American babies?
3. What is the main reason that families from Canada and Europe choose to adopt in the United States, according to the author?

Adrian Stokkeland, a 2-year-old in Canada, dances with his mom to the music of Elvis and sleeps with his most treasured possession, a box of toy cars. Emma Sonnenschein, an energetic 19-month-old in Germany, loves to "help" her mom around the house. Elisa van Meurs, a 5-year-old in the Netherlands, is a real girly-girl. Her favorite outfit is a Minnie Mouse dress, paired with a Snow White tiara and pink Barbie shoes.

Adrian, Emma, and Elisa have more in common than their charm and being the apple of their parents' eyes. All are black children born in the United States and adopted as infants by parents in other countries.

They also are representatives of a little-known trend: At the same time the US is "importing" increasing numbers of adoptive children from Russia, China, and Guatemala, it is "exporting" black babies to be adopted in other countries.

Since 1995, US State Department records indicate that international adoptions by Americans have increased more than 140 percent. Couples often cite the lack of American babies as the reason for adopting from abroad.

But the US is now the fourth largest "supplier" of babies for adoption to Canada. Adoption by Shepherd Care, an agency in Hollywood, Fla., places 90 percent of its African-American babies in Canada. One-third of the children placed through Adoption-Link in Chicago, which specializes in adoptions for black babies, go to people from other countries.

The exact numbers are not available, but interviews with adoption agencies and families in Canada, Germany, France, and the Netherlands indicate that the US also sends babies to those four countries as well as

Belgium and England. Most of the children are black newborns. Most of the adopting parents are Caucasian.

Why Is It Happening?

There is no simple explanation for why many white Americans prefer to adopt from abroad rather than adopt the available black babies at home. Racism is one reason, says Cheryl Kinnaird of Adoption-Link in Chicago. But there are others, she adds.

Families might choose an international adoption because of an affinity for a particular country or a desire to help. Many couples want a child who resembles them so that their family will not stand out as an "adoptive family." Since most adoptive families are Caucasian, this might explain the rise in adoptions from Russia and other eastern European countries.

In 2003, 37 percent of all international adoptions to the US were from countries where the majority of children adopted were Caucasian.

White couples may also be concerned about how their extended family will react to a black child. And they sometimes worry they are not up to the task of raising a black child in America and are not sure it is in the best interest of the child to be raised in a white environment.

Then, too, whites often are uncertain whether they can provide the child with cultural exposure to the African-American community.

Most adoption professionals agree that, all other things being equal, it is best to place an African-American child with an African-American family. The National Association of Black Social Workers' position is that every effort should be made to place children with families of the same race and culture.

Most, but not all, birth mothers agree, if they have the choice. However, they do not often have the choice, since fewer African-American couples apply to adoption agencies. One reason is that babies are frequently available within their extended family or community, and they have no need to go through the expense of an agency to adopt. Also, the number of infertile black couples who can afford to adopt is simply not as large as the number of black babies available.

The Word Hasn't Gotten Out

Some speculate that African-American babies have lagged behind in adoption rates because many Americans don't realize they're available. Media coverage and popular culture have focused on Americans adopting internationally rather than domestically.

"When we started to think about adoption, we thought only of international adoption because that's all we were hearing about," says Lisa Malaquin-Prey of North Carolina, mother of an adopted Russian baby. "We thought it would cost too much and that we would have to wait for a long time if we adopted domestically."

"I think that more Americans would adopt these babies if they knew they were available," says Stacy Hyer, a white American living in Germany with two adopted black children.

There is evidence of increasing adoption of black babies by white American families. But ingrained preferences still play a part in who is chosen for adoption.

A Look at Transracial Adoption

Most children are adopted by households of the same race. Percentages in chart below are based on white households with adopted children in 2000.

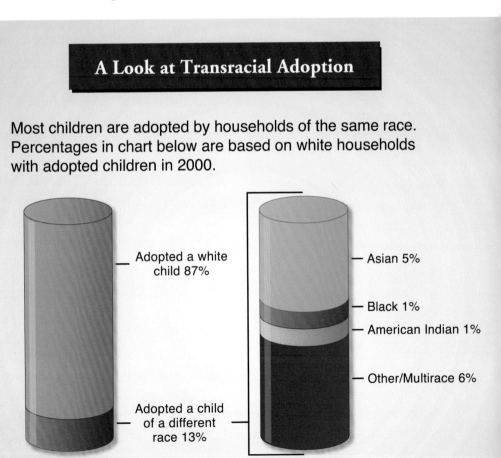

Adopted a white child 87%

Adopted a child of a different race 13%

Asian 5%

Black 1%

American Indian 1%

Other/Multirace 6%

Taken from: *New York Times*, August 17, 2006.

The majority of couples seeking to adopt are white, but there aren't nearly enough Caucasian babies available in the US to meet the demand. Although exceptions certainly exist, American parents generally prefer babies to toddlers, girls to boys, and Caucasians to African-Americans, adoption professionals report. Other ethnicities fall in between, depending on their skin color. African-American boys are at the bottom of this "ranking" system, they say, which is why they're harder to place.

"We have to work much harder to find homes for our African-American babies," says Robert Springer of Christian Homes, an adoption agency in Texas.

No one is equating babies with commodities, but the principles of supply and demand apply. Adoption costs and waiting times in the US vary depending on a baby's ranking in the "desirability list."

The Price of Babies

The children who are in the greatest demand are also in the shortest supply. Those who want to adopt healthy white babies in the US may wait as long as five years, agencies say. In contrast, they add, the waiting for African-Americans is often measured in weeks and months, especially for baby boys.

The demand for biracial (black/white) babies falls in between, and the wait reflects this. The waiting period for a biracial girl can be more than a year.

It's also the case that adopting a white baby costs more than adopting a black or biracial one.

Adoption fees for healthy Caucasian babies can be as high as $40,000, according to the US Department of Health and Human Services. For biracial babies, the cost is about $18,000. For African-American newborns, it ranges from $10,000 to $12,000, agencies say.

The costs to the adoption agency for each child also vary greatly, not because of race but due to circumstances. The agency may have

FAST FACT

For the month of January 2006, the AdoptUsKids Web site featured children available for adoptions, where 46 percent were African American, 37 percent were white, and 15 percent were Hispanic or Latino.

paid all the prenatal expenses and living costs for one birth mother, for instance, and not another, who decided on adoption in her ninth month of pregnancy.

But instead of passing along the actual costs to the new parents, many adoption agencies—most of which are nonprofit—charge a set fee that is determined by how difficult the baby may be to place. The agencies say this enables them to find homes for the children who are hardest to place.

Fees and waiting times for American families adopting internationally vary by country, but total costs, including travel, are usually about $30,000, with a waiting time of nine to 18 months.

Because of regulations and laws in the country of origin, most of the foreign children adopted from abroad by Americans are more than 1 year old when they arrive in the US.

In contrast, American babies can be adopted as soon as their parents relinquish them.

Reasons for Foreign Adoptions

Families in foreign countries cite the availability of newborns as the primary reason they choose to adopt in the US. Canada and Europe don't have as many babies available for adoption. Therefore, "if you want a newborn, you go to America," says Bart van Meurs, Elisa's dad. Families also cite the health of the babies, the short waiting time, and the availability of medical records as additional advantages. Race is seldom a consideration.

"Most of our families just want a baby as young as possible, and the US is the best place to go for a newborn," explains Lorne Welwood of Hope Adoption Services in Abbotsford, British Columbia. "They are not ignoring the race issues, but they don't think, like the Americans, that the less black the better."

"The families from abroad do not think of black babies as being second best, babies that they'll 'settle' for because white babies are hard to find," says Ms. Kinnaird.

Most adoption agencies encourage the birth mother to select the adoptive family for her child. Sometimes a black birth mother prefers having her child adopted overseas because she believes there is less prejudice there than in the US.

Many black American babies are adopted by families in foreign countries.

"Some birth mothers view placing their child abroad as a way for them to have a better life with less struggle," says Joe Sica of Shepherd Care in Hollywood, Fla.

Long-term studies of black children adopted by white parents paint a picture of well-adjusted children and teens strongly bonded to their families.

Tianna Broad, who's 12, readily fits into this picture. She's into makeup, clothes, soccer, and horses, as are most of her friends in British Columbia. "She's pretty much a typical Canadian teen," says her mother, Karen Madeiros.

Most parents abroad report little prejudice against their adopted black children. "Canada doesn't have the same race history as the US," notes Dawn Stokkeland, Adrian's Elvis-rocking mom. "There isn't the 'us' versus 'them' mentality here."

There are also not the numbers of blacks in Canada. "In my son's elementary school [in British Columbia], there are only eight blacks out of 450 kids and even fewer in my daughter's middle school," says Ms. Madeiros. "Most of the blacks here are middle-class professionals, and our neighborhoods are completely integrated."

"For the most part Germans have very positive views of blacks—they see them as singers, actors, and athletes—all positive images," explains Ms. Hyer. "My children are almost always accepted for who they are without any expectation of who they should be because of the color of their skin."

"I think the main reason there is little prejudice against blacks in Germany is because there are so few blacks here," says Peter Sonnenschein, father of two black children.

That's not to say there are never problems. Some parents say their children have encountered racism.

"Because Holland had many colonies, many [black] people live here and there is prejudice against them," says van Meurs.

"Although my [12-year-old] daughter has never experienced any racism that I know of, I can't say the same for my [10-year-old] son," says Madeiros.

Parents in Canada, Germany, and the Netherlands have formed support groups to help their children develop a positive self-image.

Signs of Change

While the news may be encouraging for African-American children adopted abroad, there's evidence of change on the home front, too, as more white Americans look into adopting black babies.

Since the US doesn't keep statistics on private domestic adoptions, the exact numbers of trans-racial adoptions are not known, but anecdotal evidence abounds of a shift toward black infants being placed with white American families.

"We can find homes for all our babies in the US, but there are regional differences," notes Robert Springer of Christian Homes in Texas, who adds that "many families in the Northeast, Northwest, and Minnesota are eager to adopt African-American babies."

Dick Van Deelen, with Adoption Associates in Michigan, reports that for the first time in 35 years they have a list of white families waiting to adopt black babies.

In a twist to the import/export world of international adoption, "We are thinking of looking to Africa to bring over more children to meet this need," he says.

Adoption-Link, in Chicago, also has a waiting list of families for black babies.

"The younger generation that is now adopting is less prejudiced and more open to becoming a mixed-race family," says Mr. Van Deelen.

Some say that the growing willingness of Americans to adopt US babies regardless of skin color comes at a good time, since placement of American babies abroad may be threatened by new regulations.

The US is in the process of ratifying an international treaty on international adoption. Although the regulations are not final, it is expected that they will make it harder for agencies to place American babies abroad.

But all the talk of adoption trends and prejudice fades in the day-to-day existence of parenting after the child arrives.

Ms. Stokkeland sums up what most parents feel. After a particularly trying day with a strong-willed 2-year-old, she sighs and says, "I wouldn't trade [Adrian] for the world. He is truly the child God wanted me to have."

The adoption was such a success that Stokkeland did it again. Earlier this month, Adrian got a new little sister, as Claire Lisa, also African-American, came north from Georgia to join him and his mother in Canada. Stokkeland says she couldn't feel more blessed.

EVALUATING THE AUTHOR'S ARGUMENTS:

In this viewpoint Dawn Davenport notes the widespread unwillingness of Americans to adopt outside of their own race, particularly as it applies to whites adopting blacks. Do you think that more white families should be willing to adopt nonwhite children? Why or why not?

Transracial Adoption of African American Children Is Not Needed

Sydney Duncan

"African American families are continually waiting, desperately hoping to adopt young black children."

In the following viewpoint Sydney Duncan claims that there are many myths and stereotypes about black families and adoption; in particular, the myth that there are not enough black families willing to adopt black children. Some of the other myths that help to support this false belief about adoption, she claims, are perceptions about how black families are faring and why black children are disproportionately represented in the child welfare system. From 1969 to 2001 Duncan held the leadership role at Homes for Black Children in Detroit, Michigan—the first specialized African American adoption agency in the United States.

Sydney Duncan, "Black Adoption Myths and Realities," *Adoptalk,* Summer 2005. Reproduced by permission.

AS YOU READ, CONSIDER THE FOLLOWING QUESTIONS:
  1. According to Duncan, what is the reason that a large percentage of children in foster care are African American?
  2. In the past, how have traditional child welfare agencies treated black children who enter the child welfare system, according to the author?
  3. What, according to Duncan, perpetuates the myth that there are not enough African American families available to adopt African American children?

Over the past 36 years, while promoting adoption opportunities for African American children, I have come to realize the depth of myths and stereotypes about black families and adoptions. Misconceptions flourish today largely because of negative and distorted media images, as well as the racial divide that continues to separate black and white communities. My purpose here is to challenge and try to correct some of the misperceptions about African Americans and African American families that greatly influence how we are viewed in relation to adoption.

African American Families Vary Greatly

While some may believe that all African American families are alike, it is important to realize that the African American community is very diverse. In fact, social and economic disparity within the black population is greater today than ever before and the chasm between the ends of the spectrum is growing steadily wider.

For most African American families, life is reasonably good and, for some, it continues to improve. For the most part, their children are staying in school, staying out of trouble, and seizing opportunities to attend college and continue on to make their mark in the world.

By contrast, a minority of African American families live in poverty in urban ghettos with little hope of change. Conditions have worsened there, and prospects for a better life are dimmer than ever. In a sense, these families have never overcome the damage of slavery, Jim Crow, and subtle forms of discrimination that still exist.

In between are families who border on poverty, but eke out a living through low paying service industry jobs, and maintain crucial community and church ties. These working poor families, often headed by single women, have achievement values and high aspirations for their children—many of whom grow up and graduate from college. Unfortunately, however, too many of these families are losing children to the streets and sons to violence.

African American Families Are Strong and Stable

Contrary to the pervasive image of broken black families struggling in urban slums, the majority of African American families, let me repeat, are well and thriving. Less than 140 years out of slavery, and only two generations removed from the legal racism of Jim Crow laws, most black families earn incomes above the poverty line. Though generally less affluent than their white counterparts, fully 40 percent of African Americans have climbed into the middle and lower middle classes in the decades since the 1960s' civil rights movement.

Where do stable black families come from? Many are descended from those who came north to work in factories and steel mills during the first half of the 20th century. Jobs available to black workers were often physically difficult, demeaning, and didn't take advantage of their skills, but the pay was better than what the rural south offered. Once these workers' families obtained an economic foothold in their new communities, they reached back to help other family members and friends move north, and started planning for their children's future.

FAST FACT

The Multiethnic Placement Act of 1994 prevents child welfare agencies that receive federal assistance from denying or delaying an application for adoption solely on the basis of race or national origin.

Others in this stable majority, often through parents' sacrifices, found better educational and employment opportunities in the post civil rights era of the 1960s. They are the beneficiaries of desegregation and an expanding economy.

Historically, African Americans' desire to give the next generation better opportunities, even at their own expense, allowed many to progress and start to realize the American dream. I think, for instance, about my grandmother who in 1910 worked as a live-in servant making $2.50 a month. She used every dime of her wage to provide my mother with a good education. This initial sacrifice, made more than 90 years ago, is part of the foundation and values on which my achievements and the achievements of my children are predicated.

African American Children Enter Foster Care Because of Poverty and Drugs

The common denominator in African American families whose children swell the ranks of foster care is poverty, not abuse as many think. According to a study published by Leroy Pelton in 1989 and confirmed by more recent studies, a family's lack of income is the single best predictor of child removal and out-of-home placement.

How a people fare has a lot to do with the economy and opportunity. Ample opportunity and a good economy help to shape positive attitudes and behaviors. In the same way, a poor economy and the absence of alternatives erodes the human spirit, destroys hope, and impairs one's ability to resist the lure of chemicals that temporarily relieve a user from the constant misery of despair.

When well-paying manufacturing jobs disappeared in the 1980s and early 1990s and drug use in depressed urban centers began to rise, poor black neighborhoods were completely destabilized. Families already dispirited by poverty watched drug traffickers moving into vacant houses and could see no light at the end of the tunnel for themselves or their children. No viable support systems were available to lift them out of poverty or remove them from the toxic environment of drug trafficking and addiction.

As we might expect, due to the disparity in incomes and opportunities between whites and blacks, and between different groups of African Americans, almost all black children we see in the child welfare system come from a minority of African American families who are in the most dire straits.

The African American Community Responds to Its Children's Needs

Due to the disproportionately large number of black children in foster care, some believe that the African American community is not dedi-

Among black families there is a long tradition of welcoming relatives' and friends' children permanently into their families.

cated to providing care for the neediest of its children. In fact, quite the opposite is true.

For more than two centuries, African American families have supported children in need by providing informal child care and foster care, and by welcoming relatives' or friends' children permanently into their families. The tradition of taking in needy or abandoned nieces, nephews, and grandchildren exists to this day, as evidenced by the high rate of informal and formal kinship care and adoption.

When Homes for Black Children formed 36 years ago, traditional child welfare agencies put almost every black child who entered the child welfare system into long-term foster care. Newborns were considered unadoptable (many workers did not believe any other African American family would want them) and workers did little to reunify children and birth parents.

At the same time, most African Americans did not even know these children were in the system. Very few worked in child welfare and white workers generally knew very little about stable African American families or their potential as resources for the children. When the first story about Homes for Black Children and the need for adoptive families was published, there came a deluge of responses from African American families interested in adopting.

Agencies Created

Inspired by Homes for Black Children's initial success, a solid network of specialized agencies, founded and led by African Americans, has responded to our children's needs in the past few decades. Based in Los Angeles County, the Institute for Black Parenting is the largest of the black adoption agencies. It was founded in 1976 by a local chapter of the Association of Black Social Workers under the leadership of Zena Oglesby and Cynthia Willard.

In 1980, Father George Clements started the first One Church, One Child program. Father Clements, who recognized the importance of and strength in black church traditions, rallied the African American religious community to promote adoption one congregation at a time. Through a federal grant awarded in 2003, the National Network of Adoption Advocacy Programs (NNAAP) was formed to promote and enhance faith-based adoption efforts modeled on the One Church, One Child program.

Other black agencies include the ROOTS Adoption Agency in Atlanta, Mississippi Families for Kids, Another Choice for Black Children in North Carolina, and REJOICE! Inc. in Harrisburg, Pennsylvania. ROOTS was incorporated in 1992 under the able leadership of Toni Oliver, an expert in training and preparing families for adoption. Mississippi Families for Kids is headed by former NACAC board president Linda West, and the nationally acclaimed Another Choice, which opened in 1995, has the dynamic Ruth Amerson at the helm. REJOICE!, a newer agency formed in 1998, is already having success placing and supporting teens.

African American Families Are Willing and Able to Adopt

At the time Homes for Black Children was formed, the prevailing belief in child welfare was that African American families were poor and already had as many or more children than they could afford. For some, that belief remains. We, however, knew that there were black families who were financially, emotionally, and spiritually capable of adopting. We knew about families who postponed having children to build a solid economic foundation for their lives, and then found they could not give birth.

In our first six months of operation, more than 700 families from across the U.S. called or wrote to us about adopting. In our first year, with a staff of six, Homes for Black Children placed 135 African American children in adoptive homes—more than the other 13 metro Detroit child welfare agencies combined.

These days Homes for Black Children, now very capably led by Jacquelynn Moffett, focuses much of its work on family preservation and prevention efforts. Even so, the adoption program—which Linda Lipscomb (formerly Whitfield) heads—still averages 40 completed adoptions per year, including placements for older children, sibling groups, and children in residential settings. In addition, about 20

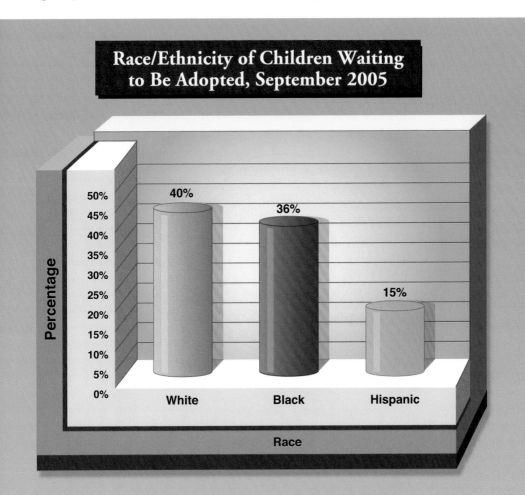

Taken from: U.S. Department of Health and Human Services, Administration for Children and Families, Administration on Children, Youth and Families, Children's Bureau, AFCARS Report, September 2006.

approved African American families are continually waiting, desperately hoping to adopt young black children.

Other African American adoption agencies have similar pools of waiting families, so I am deeply saddened when I hear of agencies sending young black children to other countries for adoption because they believe there are no African American families who would adopt them. I am even more saddened to know that someday these children may grow up to believe that no one who looked like them wanted to take care of them.

The perpetuation of this myth, I believe, is the result of looking at adoption as a service to families (who must then bear the brunt of the cost) rather than a service to children. Put another way, it is all about the money.

Almost all forward thinking agencies strongly believe that adoption is a service to the child and, as such, the cost must be a public responsibility. Adoptive families are resources for children, and when we move away from this understanding, children start to become commodities. Given African Americans' history of having been bought and sold during slavery, the thought of an agency selling (or a family buying) a black child today is understandably abhorrent. To protect our children, adoption must be viewed, and financed, as a service to the child.

Overcoming Myths About Black Adoption

Slavery and Jim Crow are difficult facts of life for American descendants of Africans. But to define us only in relation to the oppression we suffered, or those who became casualties of that oppression, is to ignore our vibrant life, strengths, and values. These are our realities:

- Most African American families are making a decent life for themselves and their children. They find support and comfort in family, community, and church.
- When black children enter foster care, extreme poverty and drug use are the most common underlying causes.
- Recognizing the plight of African American children without parents, black families have been responding to and helping children for centuries. Over the past three plus decades, a network of African American adoption agencies has also dedicated itself to finding homes for children of color.

- When adoption is presented as a service to children, and recruitment efforts involve and reach sensitively into the black community, African American families will come forward to adopt.

There are yet many challenges that African American families and children must confront and overcome. But the broader community must not ignore black families' strength, determination, and capacity to care for African American children. Our dreams live in our hopes for our children, and I believe that our families' strengths will continue to fuel new and healing child welfare practices for children of color.

EVALUATING THE AUTHOR'S ARGUMENTS:

In this viewpoint Sydney Duncan argues that there are African American families able to adopt black American children. If there are available families, do you think it ought to effect the ability of black American children to be adopted abroad, such as the adoptions described in the previous viewpoint?

International Adoption Should Be Encouraged

"No matter what Madonna's motives are, she is doing the right thing."

Cynthia Tucker

In the following viewpoint Cynthia Tucker argues that international adoptions, such as Madonna's adoption of a one-year-old boy from Malawi, should be encouraged. Tucker denounces the accusations that Madonna is adopting a child on a whim, noting that the recent popularity, or so-called trend, of adoption of children from developing countries is a good thing. The needs of children in the developing world are immense, Tucker claims, and adoption is one way to help. Tucker is a columnist for the *Atlanta Journal-Constitution*.

AS YOU READ, CONSIDER THE FOLLOWING QUESTIONS:

1. According to Tucker, what is the situation in Malawi that has created such great need for adoption and other help?
2. What criticism did Madonna draw from human rights groups in Malawi, according to the author?
3. How does the author respond to critics who think that instead of adoption, money should be sent to Malawi and other developing nations to allow parents to keep their children?

Thank heaven for Oprah. Last week [October 2006], the queen of TV talk had the clear-eyed common sense to applaud Madonna's charitable works in the desperately poor African nation of Malawi. Interviewing the beleaguered pop culture icon via satellite, Oprah made clear that she and her studio audience supported Madonna's efforts, including her provisional adoption of a small boy.

In Praise of Madonna's Adoption

It's about time that an influential voice stepped forward to state the obvious: No matter what Madonna's motives are, she is doing the right thing. Malawi, a small nation in the southeast corner of the continent, is struggling with drought, beset by malaria and ravaged by AIDS. An estimated 14 percent of adults have been infected with HIV, and nearly 1 million children have lost at least one parent to the disease.

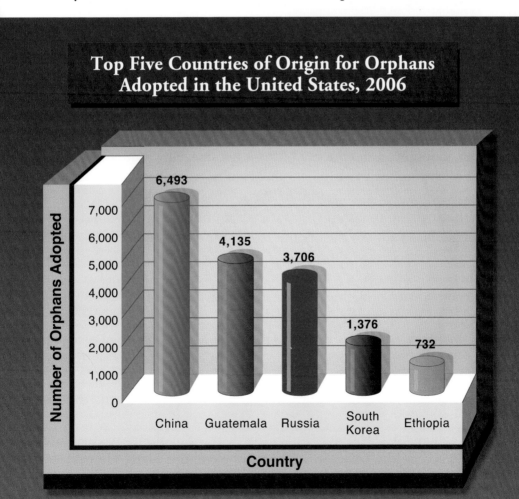

Taken from: U.S. Department of State, "Immigrant Visas Issued to Orphans Coming to the U.S.," http://travel.state.gov.

Working with developing-world economist Jeffrey Sachs, Madonna has pledged to raise $3 million for anti-poverty efforts in Malawi. So orphanages will receive money for food and medicine; villages may get clean water and provisions for fighting malaria; and, if the adoption goes through, a toddler born into unfathomable poverty will be reared in immeasurable affluence. That's a bad thing?

With the tsunami of depressing developments that have dominated the news recently—genocide in Darfur, nuclear tests in North Korea, savagery in Baghdad—you'd think that Madonna's good works would be cause for celebration. Think again.

Criticism of Madonna

In the month or so since she visited Malawi [in 2006] and news leaked of her planned adoption, she has been swamped by a tide of cynicism, opprobrium and controversy. Pop culture critics have derided her adoption as an effort to burnish her image by joining the ranks of celebrities such as U.N. goodwill ambassador Angelina Jolie, who has adopted two children from the developing world.

Human rights groups in Malawi announced they would challenge the legality of the adoption, claiming Madonna's money and fame allowed her to short-circuit traditional procedures. Worse still, there were reports last week that Yohane Banda—father of year-old David—had claimed government officials tricked him into signing papers forfeiting his parental rights.

Banda has since told reporters that he has no intention of reneging on the adoption. "These so-called human rights activists are harassing me every day, threatening me that I am not aware of what I am doing," Banda said, adding that he was worried that all the controversy might cause Madonna to change her mind.

"I'm afraid David may be sent back and the orphanage may not even accept him back. So where will he end up? Here? He will certainly die," he said, according to The Associated Press. (His wife and two other children died, reportedly from malaria.)

Adoptions and Other Charity Are Needed

It may well be that those "so-called human rights activists"—aptly put—simply oppose foreign adoptions. Their narrow-mindedness is reminiscent of outspoken black American social workers, many of whom worked for years to prevent interracial adoptions, preferring to see black children languish in orphanages or foster homes rather than be adopted by white parents.

As for the claims of some critics that celebrity adoptions are simply the latest "fashion," so what? That's a trend that holds more promise than the purchase of overpriced handbags, cosmetic surgery and leaked videos of sexual escapades. If it's a publicity gimmick, it will do more for needy children than inviting millions of strangers to observe their personal lives on "reality" TV.

Yohane Banda, father of Madonna's adopted child, speaks to reporters about the harassment he has received from human rights advocates.

After the fall of the Soviet Union, the United States virtually abandoned Africa because it no longer held strategic value. Since then, the continent's most effective advocate has been Bono, the Irish rock star, who has spent years campaigning for debt relief and anti-poverty programs. If he has persuaded other celebrities to join the cause, God bless him.

If you think Madonna should have given Banda money to keep his own child, then perhaps you should consider an organization that helps parents support their kids. For $50 a month, my mother helps to support a 10-year-old Senegalese child, Binta, by sending a check to World Vision religiously. Countless other agencies, including the United Nations Children's Fund—one of my favorite charities—are doing good work in the developing world.

And if you believe there are a host of children right here in the United States waiting for a good home, you're right. Foster parents, especially, are always in short supply.

Rather than a wave of criticism, Madonna's gutsy move should have provoked a tide of donations to charities for needy children.

EVALUATING THE AUTHOR'S ARGUMENTS:

In this viewpoint the author claims that people who adopt needy children from the developing world, such as Madonna, ought to be commended. Name one reason that critics may claim that aid, and not adoption, is a preferable solution.

International Adoption Should Not Be Encouraged

Mirah Riben

> *"We need to stop glamorizing foreign adoption as a rescue mission."*

In the following viewpoint Mirah Riben argues that there are many problems with international adoption. Riben claims that the different countries from which Westerners adopt over time follow patterns of unrest in the developing world, raising a concern about the corruption involved in such adoptions. Additionally, Riben faults the current adoption model as overly commercial and calls for a change in thinking about adoption that focuses on keeping families together. Riben is the author of *The Stork Market: America's Multi-Billion Dollar Unregulated Adoption Industry* and *Shedding Light on . . . the Dark Side of Adoption.*

AS YOU READ, CONSIDER THE FOLLOWING QUESTIONS:
1. According to the author, what has led to an increase in international adoptions?
2. Why have thirteen countries suspended or ended their adoption programs in recent years, according to Riben?
3. Riben claims what negative consequence in the United States is the result of international adoption?

Mirah Riben, "Big Business in Babies: Adoption, the Child Commodities Market," countercurrent.org, April 25, 2007. Reproduced by permission of the author.

Adoption was once a process by which the community took responsibility for orphans. Increased access to birth control pills and legal abortion, and a lessening of the stigma of single parenting, coupled with an increase in infertility resulted in a demand for babies that outstrips the "supply." And where there is demand—be it for diamonds, drugs, sex, or babies—corruption follows.

International Adoption Trends Follow Unrest

Adoption is racist. The scarcity of "white American-born babies" has led to an increase in international adoptions, fracturing family ties and heritage in what some are calling cultural genocide. Madonna was criticized. Angelina confounds. Westerners, however, continue to believe that adoption "rescues" orphans; though saving children from poverty, one at a time, does nothing to ameliorate the conditions that continue to produce them. And, many so-called orphans are in fact stolen, kidnapped, or their parents were coerced to relinquish them under false pretenses to be sold on the black and gray adoption markets with prices set by age, alleged health, skin color, gender and nationality.

As Americans import mostly light-skinned babies, non-white children are left behind, and the number of black, American-born babies adopted by overseas families has increased significantly in recent years, with

Signe Wilkinson Editorial Cartoon © 2006 Signe Wilkinson. All rights reserved. Used with the permission of Signe Wilkinson and the Washington Post Writers Group in conjunction with the Cartoonist Group.

black babies being placed with Canadian couples more than ever before. Adoption trends follow poverty and sociopolitical upheaval from Latin America to Asia and Eastern Europe. Since the 1990s, China and Russia have become the largest exporters of children for international adoption. Unrest and poverty in these nations makes them ripe for corruption and trafficking. In April 2007, the U.S. State Department confirmed that Guatemalan babies are kidnapped for adoption and other mothers pressured to sell their babies by corrupt, inadequately supervised notaries. The previous month, a Utah adoption agency was indicted for "systematically misleading birth parents in Samoa into signing away rights to their children while telling

FAST FACT

The number of international adoptions, based on the number of immigrant visas issued to orphans, nearly doubled from 10,641 in 1996 to 20,679 in 2006, according to the U.S. Department of State.

adoptive parents in the United States that the children had been abandoned and were orphans." All of this while UNICEF is investigating child trafficking and babies being sold for adoption in Nepal.

As abuses are exposed, countries are restricting out-of-country adoption of their children. According to Ethica, a nonprofit adoption advocacy organization, 13 countries have suspended or ended their adoption programs in the past 15 years and four more countries temporarily stopped adoptions to investigate allegations of corruption or child trafficking. The U.S. passage of the 2005 Trafficking Victim Protection Reauthorization Act verified recognition of international adoption providing an incentive for child trafficking. Yet, ethnocentricity and a national policy of spreading democracy and the American way of life to the world, combined with a desire to parent, continues the romanticized "rescue" myth. . . .

The Negative Effects of International Adoption

Adoption, which was a means of providing care for children who needed it, has become a perverse business of providing children for those who feel entitled to one. Consumerism has led many westerners, particularly Americans, to believe that if they can afford "it" they

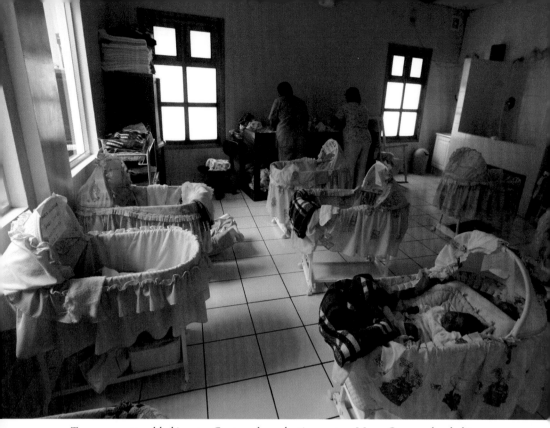

Two nurses attend babies at a Guatemalan adoption center. Many Guatemalan babies are kidnapped for adoption, and mothers have been pressured to sell their babies to corrupt officials.

deserve to have "it"—even when "it" is a human child. Adoption needs to return to basics. We need to halt profiteering from what should be a social service to protect families and children in need. Adoption can only guarantee a different life, not necessarily a "better" one. Adoption moves children from lower to higher socio-economic status, yet even when a child is adopted into a loving, caring family who may provide a more prosperous lifestyle—the end result does not justify the means if the child was kidnapped, stolen or their mothers coerced, deceived or exploited. Adoptions that obliterate a person's original identity and leave him no legal access to his family are a risk and a violation of human rights as expressed by UNICEF.

All adoptions are not the happily-ever-after fairy tales we'd like them to be. Many are sad and sordid. For this reason we need to stop promoting "adoption" without distinguishing between those that are necessary and in the best interest of children and are handled ethically—from those which are not. The former deserves support; the latter needs to be exposed and ended. We need to stop glamorizing foreign adoption as a rescue mission but recognize that every international adoption leaves behind half a million children in U.S. foster care. Of those, 134,000 children cannot be reclaimed by family members. Adoptions of such children only are worthy of promoting and financial aiding in the form of taxes and other incentives and benefits. Monies paid to non-relative foster parents would be better spent to preserve, maintain and protect the integrity of families in need, including aid to grandparents and other extended family members struggling to keep families intact. Additionally, the U.S. ought to consider a tax on international adoptions with funds used to support families and children in the U.S. in crisis.

Adoption needs to be far more transparent, open, honest and regulated to ensure it serves the best interest of those it is intended to serve.

EVALUATING THE AUTHORS' ARGUMENTS:

In this viewpoint Mirah Riben decries the practice of international adoption. What do you think Cynthia Tucker, author of the previous viewpoint, would say in response to Riben's claim that many international adoptions involve corruption and the violation of human rights?

Chapter 3

What Policies Should Govern Adoption?

An orphanage worker cares for babies in San Jose Pinulqa, Guatemala. Many foreign countries, like Guatemala, have become much more open in releasing adoption records.

Adoption Records Should Always Be Available to Adult Adoptees

Lorraine Dusky

"The impassioned pleas of adoptees asking for open records are nearly drowned out."

In the following viewpoint Lorraine Dusky argues that adoptees should have access to records about their birth, which name their birth parents. Dusky contends that the argument for anonymity of birth parents is outdated and unwanted. Appealing to the rights of adoptees to know their origin, Dusky supports the view that records be open even in the case of birth parents who desire anonymity, though she sympathizes with their desire. Lorraine Dusky is the author of *Birthmark*, a memoir about surrendering her daughter to adoption.

AS YOU READ, CONSIDER THE FOLLOWING QUESTIONS:

1. According to Dusky, why are open birth records important to adoptees?
2. What does the author identify as the reason for opposition to changing laws to enable open records for adoptees?
3. What evidence does the author give in support of the claim that few birth parents desire anonymity?

Lorraine Dusky, "Birth Mothers, Adoptees Have Right to Records," *Women's eNews*, December 29, 2004. Reproduced by permission.

On Monday [January 3, 2005], Janet Allen plans to walk into the Division of Vital Records Administration in Concord, N.H., and ask for a copy of her original birth certificate. It will be the first time she can legally obtain it.

Allen, 51, a state legislator, was adopted as an infant. In New Hampshire, where she was born and adopted, Allen has been denied the right to that singular piece of paper that contains the answer to one of life's most basic questions: Who am I? The change in the law occurs two days from now, New Years Day, 2005. As one of the people who worked for the bill's passage, Allen will be first in line.

"I am no longer a child and am delighted to finally have the same rights as non-adopted adults," she says. "The law now guarantees that no one will ever again have to go before a judge to beg, plead and be humiliated for a piece of paper that belongs to him."

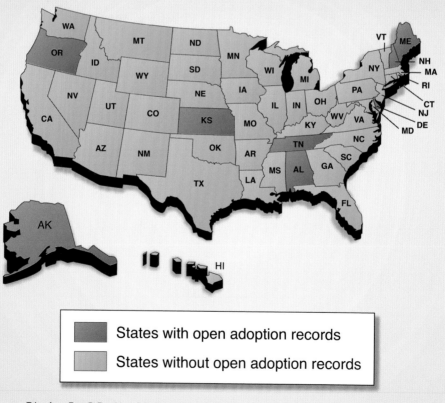

States with Open Records for Adult Adoptees, 2007

- States with open adoption records
- States without open adoption records

Taken from: Evan B. Donaldson Adoption Institute, "For the Records: Restoring a Right to Adult Adoptees," November 2007.

Why does it matter so much to her and thousands of other adopted people in the state? Because her original birth certificate—not the amended one she's had most of her life—contains the names of her birth parents, and thus the key to her identity and origin. With the names, adopted people can search out their natural parents and perhaps obtain not only answers, but also updated medical information as well, as the possibility of an ongoing relationship.

States with Open Records

With the law's passage, New Hampshire joined six other states—Alabama, Alaska, Delaware, Kansas, Tennessee and Oregon—that allow individuals adopted as children the right to their original birth certificates.

Some states had open birth records until the 1960s and even into 1980s. But as adoption became more common following the sexual revolution of those times, most of the states left with open records closed them, sweeping aside the rights of adopted children, no matter their age, to investigate their origins.

FAST FACT

For many adoptees, their original birth certificates with birth parent names are replaced with birth certificates that reflect the names of adoptive parents.

The bills to modernize the laws encounter stiff opposition and intense lobbying in state legislatures everywhere from adoption agencies and attorneys, local Catholic charities, the Church of Jesus Christ of Latter-Day Saints, and state chapters of the American Civil Liberties Union.

Against these well-funded organizations, the impassioned pleas of adoptees asking for open records are nearly drowned out, even though they are the ones whose rights should be tantamount.

In numerous states, bills to open the records have either languished in committee or died at the end of a legislative session. The opposition always hinges on the supposed anonymity that the women who gave up their children 30, 40 years ago were promised then, and are said to fervently desire today.

Not All Birth Mothers Want Anonymity

I am one of those women, and I was not "promised" anonymity from my daughter. It was forced on me like a pair of manacles. The relinquishment papers gave me no opportunity to confirm or deny whether I might want to know her one day. There were no boxes to check marked either "contact desired" or "no contact." The papers merely stated that I was turning over my daughter to the state. The document promised nothing, not even that she would be adopted.

Our forced anonymity is a by-product of laws that seal the original birth certificate from the adopted parson, designed to give adoptive parents the feeling their adopted children are really "theirs." Love was expected to quell curiosity. We birth mothers were supposed to "get on with our lives."

I protested to my social worker because never to know my own child sounded like living death. But I felt I had no choice; I signed the papers.

I am not alone. The vast majority of us desperately want to know our children. We pray for the knock on the door, the phone call that will begin our healing.

How many of us are there? Probably between 5 million and 6 million, given the best estimate of "stranger" adoptions, those in which the baby is not given to a family member. How many of us seek reunion? There is no accurate way to know. But data from Oregon, which has allowed adoptees access to their original birth certificates since 2000, is as good an indicator as any.

Few Check "No Contact"

As part of the new law, Oregon gave birth mothers, as well as fathers, a chance to file a "no contact" preference. Near the end of 2004, nearly 8,000 adoptees had requested and received their original birth certificates. Eighty-three birth parents had asked for no contact, just a smidgeon over 1 percent.

In New Hampshire, the group of adoptees and birth parents who fought for open records has sent an e-mail alert that has been bouncing around the Web for the last month, trying to ferret out New Hampshire birth mothers, assuming most will want to update their names and addresses so their children can find them.

Of course, there will be some who ask for no contact.

I try to sympathize with those women who want to hide from their own children. Perhaps they never told their husbands or their other children. Perhaps they have buried the secret so deeply—because it hurts too much to do otherwise—that they can not even imagine dealing with a flesh-and-blood person who asks "why?" Perhaps they are too guilty to face the child, now grown.

Attitudes Change over Time

If you knew me when my daughter was born, in 1966 in Rochester, N.Y., you might guess I would be one of them today. The father, a married man with a public life, had to be "protected." For his sake, and yes, mine, I operated in deepest secrecy. A Catholic girl a year out of college, so deep was my shame that I hid my pregnancy from my family in another state.

Workers from Lost Loved Ones, an organization that does birth certificate research, go through courthouse records to find birth certificates of adopted children.

But times and attitudes change. As far back as 1980, after holding numerous hearings around the country, the then Department of Health, Education and Welfare proposed a Model Adoption Act that would have opened the records.

"There can be no legally protected interest in keeping one's identity secret from one's biological offspring; parents and child are considered co-owners of the information regarding the event of birth," it stated. "The birth parents' interest in reputation is not alone deserving of constitutional protection." But while some provisions of the act became national policy, this did not.

I am no longer the terrified young thing I was back in 1966.

Years ago, I decided I couldn't wait for Congress, or New York's legislature, to act. I paid a searcher $1,200. Within weeks I had my daughter's name and phone number and made that scary phone call to her other mother. Our daughter was still a teen-ager. I met her and her family in a matter of days.

That was more than two decades ago.

At my daughter's wedding, I stood next to her other mother during the ceremony. Yes, I was the one who didn't know a lot of people there, but my brothers and their wives, and some of their kids, were there too. It was a happy event for everyone. It was as it should be.

EVALUATING THE AUTHOR'S ARGUMENTS:

In this viewpoint Lorraine Dusky argues that it is the right of the adopted child to have access to his or her birth certificate. What might someone argue is a competing right of the birth parent that outweighs this right?

Adoption Records Should Not Always Be Available to Adult Adoptees

"There are several ways that mandatory openness harms adoption, birthparents, children, and families."

Thomas C. Atwood

In the following viewpoint Thomas C. Atwood, of the National Council for Adoption (NCFA), gives reasons for opposing laws that make adoption records open to adult adoptees in all situations. Atwood claims there are several harms of mandatory openness, including violation of privacy of birth parents, increase in unwanted contact of birth parents, harm to the strength of the adoptive family, and increases in abortion and foster care. As such, Atwood concludes that a mutual consent registry is the best policy. Atwood is president and CEO of the NCFA, a nonprofit organization that works to promote adoption.

The issue of "open records" has been hotly debated for decades and the National Council for Adoption (NCFA) has been active in opposing the unilateral and coercive nature of those proposals. NCFA does not oppose reunions or the exchange of identifying information between mutually consenting parties to adoption. What we oppose is the law empowering one party to adoption to force himself or herself on another. . . .

Search and reunion advocacy is commonplace in the media, but views among birthparents, adopted persons, and adoptive parents regarding confidentiality and openness in adoption are actually as diverse and personal as they can be. The only just way to reconcile these varying views is through mutual consent, not unilateral coercion. . . .

Unfortunately, the loudest voices legislatures and the public generally hear regarding this issue belong to a small minority of adopted persons who insist upon an absolute right to identify and even to contact their birthparents, without birthparents' consent. . . .

It is vital for legislators who conduct hearings on this issue to recognize that they will generally hear more from proponents of "open records" than from opponents. Birthparents who prefer privacy cannot discuss their views publicly without sacrificing the very privacy they desire to protect. They must either remain mute while their rights are being taken away or lose their confidentiality in the act of defending it. If they could speak, there would be many such witnesses in those hearings, with very sympathetic and emotional testimonies. . . .

There are several ways that mandatory openness harms adoption, birthparents, children, and families:

Right to Privacy

First, mandatory openness violates birthparents' basic human right to privacy. "Open-records" policies completely eliminate birthparents' right to choose a confidential adoption, both retroactively and prospectively. To open records retroactively without the approval of a birthmother who was promised privacy is a particularly egregious violation of trust and common decency. For the typical birthmother, making an adoption plan for her child is a supremely loving act, committed in the best interests of her child. The law should honor birthmothers for this act of love, not punish them by stripping them of their basic human right to privacy.

Jack Ferns looks over his birth certificate at the Division of Vital Records in Concord, New Hampshire. A new state law allows individuals like Jack to get a copy of their birth certificate to find the name of their birth parents.

Under mandatory-openness policies, no future birthmother may choose a confidential adoption, no matter what the circumstances of pregnancy or birth, even in the cases of rape or incest. Consider this true story: One birthmother, who placed a child conceived in rape, in preparing to meet with the adult adopted child, was asked by the child to reunite with the father, too! Fortunately, because her identity had not yet been revealed, in accordance with the guidelines of the mutual consent registry in her state, she was able to withdraw from the situation and decline the reunion. A mandatory-openness policy would not have allowed her to avoid a traumatic and even dangerous situation.

Policymakers, adoption professionals, and the public should recognize that there are any number of legitimate and understandable reasons that birthparents may desire confidentiality—perhaps the birthparent does not want to upset his or her spouse, family, and friends with a never shared revelation; perhaps the birthparent is psychologically or emotionally unable or unready to handle the stress of renewed contact; perhaps the birthmother may be interested in contact some day, but needs to control the timing; perhaps the birthmother does not want to relive the abusive relationship, rape, or incest that caused the pregnancy, or fears possible contact with the birthfather; or perhaps the birthparent simply believes that the healthiest approach for all parties is not to have an ongoing relationship. It is oppressive to impose a one-size-fits-all, mandatory-openness policy, instead of respecting birthparents' loving discernment and their right to privacy. . . .

Unwanted Contact

Second, mandatory openness increases the number of unwanted, unilaterally imposed contacts between adopted persons and birthparents. Providing adult adopted persons identifying birthparent information without birthparents' knowledge or consent increases the number of unwanted, unilaterally imposed contacts. When such a law is passed in a state, many thousands of birthparents, around the state, country, and world, become vulnerable, especially because very few of them are even aware that their privacy has been eliminated. Even if they are aware of the new law, they are powerless to prevent unwanted contacts or control the timing of them. Unwanted reunions between adult adopted persons and birthparents are often highly disruptive and even traumatic for everyone involved. Even when adopted persons and birthparents mutually consent to contact, their satisfaction with reunions and ongoing relationships is quite unpredictable, despite the rosy scenarios often portrayed in the media.

Mandatory-openness advocates frequently offer a "contact preference form" as an attempt to address concerns about unwanted contacts. However, such forms are only indications of birthparent preferences and have no legally binding effect. They still allow the release of birthparents' identifying information without their consent, which is a violation of privacy in and of itself. And they still leave birthparents vulnerable to unilaterally imposed contacts, and the fear thereof, even if such contacts never occur. . . .

Undermining the Adoptive Family

Third, mandatory openness undermines the strength of the adoptive family. A chief reason adoption has been so successful is that society and law have respected the adoptive family as the child's true and permanent family. Adoption is not "long-term foster care," until the child grows up and can reunite with the "real" family. But by empowering one side to force herself or himself on the other, mandatory openness establishes the state as a reunion advocate, rather than the neutral party it should be. It establishes as the legal norm and the cultural expectation that adopted persons and their birthparents will, and should, "reunite" when the child reaches the age of majority. Such a policy not only promotes emotional and traumatic experiences in families, it sends the corrosive message that adoptive families are somehow inadequate to meet the psychological needs of their adopted members.

This message attacks a very foundation of adoption, that the adoptive family is the child's true and permanent family. Adoptive parenting has provided untold social and familial benefits to children throughout the years. Law and society must continue to respect the adoptive family as the adopted person's true and permanent family, in order for those benefits to continue.

Increases in Abortion and Foster Care

Fourth, mandatory openness reduces the confidential options available to women with unplanned pregnancies and causes some women who would otherwise choose adoption to choose abortion. There are significant numbers of women with unplanned pregnancies, who are concerned about privacy in making their decisions regarding their pregnancies. Clearly, some number of these women, who would otherwise choose adoption, would choose abortion if they could not choose adoption with the assurance of confidentiality. What that number would be is impossible to tell, but what does it need to be? The loss of human potential from even one abortion that would have been an adoption is unknowable. . . .

Fifth, mandatory openness reduces the number of adoptions and increases the number of children in foster care. Eliminating privacy in adoption would mean that women with unplanned, out-of-wedlock births, who would only choose adoption if it was confidential, would have no choice but to single-parent. Social science data clearly reveal that the more single parents there are, the more children languish in foster care, with greatly increased costs to the child, family, society, and taxpayer as a result. Forcing women to parent when they are not ready to do so leads to more children in foster care, as evidenced by the large increases in the foster care rolls that have occurred, as the number of infant adoptions dramatically declined over the last 30 years. . . .

A Fair and Effective Policy—the Mutual Consent Registry

NCFA advocates the mutual consent registry as the most equitable policy for handling the issue of openness and privacy in adoption. More than 40 states allow birthparents and adult adopted persons, who desire to exchange identifying information and/or have contact, to register with the state their interest in doing so, in which case the state informs both parties and facilitates the process. By allowing birthparents and adult adopted persons to permit or prohibit the release of their identity, the registries facilitate mutually consensual contact, while enabling the parties to safeguard their privacy, if they so choose. Some states allow birthparents to authorize at the time of placement, as part of the adoption approval process, the release or nonrelease of their identifying information to the adult adopted child upon request. Such policies respect the principle of mutual consent, so long as the birthparent may change his or her designation at any time.

A "match" in a mutual consent registry occurs when both an adult adopted person and a birthparent register with the state their interest in exchanging identifying information and/or contact. Mandatory-openness advocates often attempt to justify their opposition to mutual consent registries by stating that the low frequency of matches is evidence of the policy's ineffectiveness. But any party to adoption interested in contact learns very quickly of the existence of the registry. If an adopted person or birthparent chooses not to register at that point, the logical explanation is that the party

Percentage of Americans Who Would Be Concerned About Having an Adoptive Child Seek Out Birth Parents When Grown

No concern at all

Major concern

18%

40%

42%

Minor concern

Taken from: Harris Interactive Inc., "National Adoption Attitudes Survey," June 2002.

is simply not interested in having contact or sharing identifying information, not that the policy "doesn't work." The policy allows the parties to choose. If they do not choose the way mandatory-openness advocates think they ought, that does not mean there is something wrong with the policy. People who choose not to register should be allowed to maintain their privacy.

EVALUATING THE AUTHORS' ARGUMENTS:

In this viewpoint Thomas C. Atwood argues that having state laws that mandate open birth records for adult adoptees would result in more abortions and more children in foster care. How might the author of the previous viewpoint, Lorraine Dusky, respond to these two concerns?

Viewpoint 3

Open Adoption Is the Best Policy

Bill Betzen

"The ideal is that the birth and adoptive mothers become good friends."

In the following viewpoint Bill Betzen, writing for an audience of pregnant women considering adoption, argues that only open adoption should be considered. While Betzen believes that open adoption does not create a situation where birth parents are coparents, he does believe that ongoing contact between adopted child and birth parent(s) is best for the well-being of the child. Betzen is the creator of the Web site www.openadoption.org and a former social worker who worked in the area of child welfare, including adoption.

AS YOU READ, CONSIDER THE FOLLOWING QUESTIONS:

1. According to the author, when a birth parent is involved in an open adoption, what kind of role does the birth parent have toward the adopted child?
2. What are two of the six reasons that Betzen gives for preferring open adoption that have to do with health?
3. What is Betzen's concern about a "semi-open adoption" where all contact is mediated by the adoption agency?

Bill Betzen, "Recommendations for Parents Considering Placement of a Child," openadoption.org, December 27, 2005. Reproduced by permission.

The term "Open Adoption" is used and defined VERY differently by different agencies. Do not allow an agency to try to convince you that anything less than a fully open adoption is the best. You should have the full power to select the family you want. You should know their full identity, and meet and know them, and their home. Each of you should make a life long commitment to stay in direct contact with each other with visits at least once a year. . . .

Adoptive Families Should Prefer Open Adoption

Some agencies are what you call "Open-adoption-if-that-is-the-only-way-we-can-have-an-adoption" agencies. That is not the type of agency you want. You want an agency that has families who all emphatically want a fully open adoption for their child. They understand the value of a fully open adoption for their child and they expect a fully open adoption.

The good news is that more and more agencies every year are fully open adoption agencies wherein the birth mother can look at the resume of every family the agency has awaiting adoption. All resumes will be fully identified, not only with pictures but with full names, addresses, and home phone numbers you may call to talk with the families if you want. All of the families want and expect a fully open, ongoing relationship, adoption. Many of the resumes will be of families in our own area. That is the kind of agency you want to look for. . . .

Your placement decision needs to be as free a decision as is humanly possible. It needs to be one you can be proud of because you have searched and found a loving family nearby, a family you are getting to know well and will give to your child. A child is not given, a family is. The child should be the center of this process. All the adults involved are only there for the child's best interest.

Please be sensitive to the fact that there is a very, very, small minority of women who will pretend to be planning an adoption just to get their expenses covered. It is a sad fact that agencies, and families in independent adoption, must make every effort to protect themselves from such manipulation. Please be sensitive to that reality as you go through your adoption process. Hopefully expenses will not be a major issue for your individual adoption. That quickly eliminates this issue and it will be easier for you to decide to parent once you see that wonderful child.

A greater danger for you will be families who will promise an open adoption and then disappear as soon as the adoption is legally final. That appears to be much more common than the dishonest parents pretending to be planning adoption mentioned in the above paragraph. Please be very careful. Work with an adoption agency to help lessen the danger of your child's open adoption one day closing. . . .

What Open Adoption Is Not

In considering a fully open, ongoing relationship, adoption, please know that this will not mean that you will be seen as parent by your child. Yes, you will always be the birth parent. But the family you select will fully be "Mom" and "Dad." Open adoption does NOT mean "co-parenting." There is only one set of parents and you must be willing to fully give up that role. A birth parent often comes into a role something like a favorite aunt. It is another relative, a very important relative, but

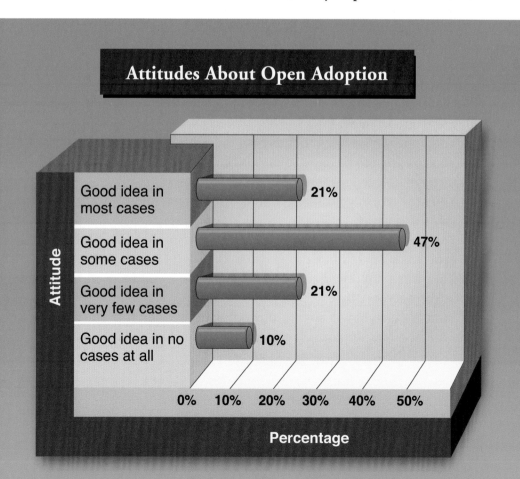

Attitudes About Open Adoption

Good idea in most cases — 21%
Good idea in some cases — 47%
Good idea in very few cases — 21%
Good idea in no cases at all — 10%

Attitude / Percentage

Taken from: Harris Interactive Inc., "National Adoption Attitudes Survey," June 2002, www.adoptioninstitute.org.

not "Mom" nor "Dad." If you do not want to give up that role in your child's life, please do not make an adoption plan.

Most importantly, open adoption will not eliminate the pain of losing your child. Yes, it is not as bad as the pain of a closed adoption, but there is still an intense loss that will never be regained. You are no longer a parent to your child.

In open adoption there is NEVER any guarantee that the adopting family will keep their side of the agreement to stay in contact. In several states there are some elements in the adoption reform movement who are working for legally enforceable open adoption agreements. I am not comfortable with legally enforcible open adoptions because I am concerned that it will be used to "sell adoption." The reality is that once a case gets into court everyone has lost, and most probably the birth family has lost the most. They often may not have the funds for a court fight. If for any reason you are hesitant to fully trust the adopting family, then do not choose adoption. This is another good reason to work with an agency. The agency is there to help you. While it is very rare there is a problem in this area, even once is too often.

Reasons for a Fully Open Adoption
1) You search for and select the family for your child. You check them out yourself.
2) You hopefully become friends with the adoptive mother and father. You continue to be in personal contact (not just letters and pictures through an agency) as your birth child grows.
3) You are there as your birth child grows and has questions that only you can answer.
4) You are there to help with any needed family research if there are genetically related health questions that develop.
5) Your birth child will always be able to give a full medical history in the doctors office.
6) Your birth child will always know of your love and that you simply wanted a family that you yourself could not provide at that time in your life.

Support for Open Adoption in Research
There are many other reasons to select open adoption that are rooted in the research that has been completed. . . .

Dr. Ruth McRoy of the University of Texas in Austin has reported that in their five year study of over 500 triad members, that children of open adoptions have a more positive image of their birth mother. My question is "What does that indicate about a child's self image, especially when compared with a child in a closed adoption?"

Adoptive parents with fully open adoptions are less fearful of the stability of their adoption, and more comfortable talking about adoption, than closed adoption parents. In an article published in *Family Process*, a professional journal, the June 1994 issue (pp. 141–142), it was reported from this same research by Dr. McRoy that:

> The strong general pattern is that parents in fully disclosed adoptions demonstrate higher degrees of empathy about adoption, talk about it more openly with their children, and are less fearful that the birth mother might try to reclaim her child than are parents in confidential adoptions. The sense of permanence in the relationship with their adopted child also followed this pattern. . . .

Dr. Marianne Berry reports from the California Longitudinal Study on Adoption (an ongoing study of 1300 people started in 1988) that children of open adoptions are reported to have fewer behavioral problems than children of closed adoptions.

Dr. Anu Sharma of the Search Institute in Minneapolis (a 35 year old non-profit family research center) reports that information issues are a major preoccupation for adolescent adoptees from closed adoptions. This was found in the process of preparing survey instruments for a national study of adolescent adoptee mental health. . . . In asking open ended questions as to the adoption related issues that concerned them most, both adoptees and their parents listed the lack of information as issues that concerned them the most. In this study 65% of adoptees wanted to meet their birth mother.

In open adoption situations, mothers like Kendra Lenz (left) often maintain contact with their children.

This was found to be true of the adolescents in this study even though adoption search experts report that the desire to search usually is not presented and acted upon until much later in life. What will happen to this 65% within the next 10 years? In 10 years will 95% of these same adoptees want to meet their birth mothers? And how many will act on that desire?

All major national adoption conferences in the U.S. are presenting open adoption practice as the healthiest adoption method for the sake of the adoptee. . . .

Openness Means Trust

If "open adoption" only means an occasional face to face meeting arranged by the agency, and letters and pictures passed through the agency, then again you need to find another agency. What does such a semi-open adoption say about the ability of the family to trust you? You have trusted them with your child and this is how they trust you? Healthy adoption can only be built on full trust. The research is in and open adoption is the healthiest for all parties involved.

Ask how many of their adoptions last year were fully open, ongoing relationship, adoptions? Hopefully it was over 50% of all adoptions. There are agencies now with over 90% of all adoptions falling into this category of excellence!

Another good test is to call to get a copy of the information an agency mails out to adopting parents. If the agency will readily accept families not wanting a fully open adoption, or even a semi-open adoption, then find another agency.

I strongly recommend that you call many adoption agencies in your area to find a fully open agency, one that will encourage you to have a fully open adoption. You should know the adopting family and they should know you. You should visit each others' homes and hopefully you will not live too far from each other. The ideal is that the birth and adoptive mothers become good friends, as well as the birth and adoptive fathers if possible. All parties will be joined by an intense interest in the child.

EVALUATING THE AUTHOR'S ARGUMENTS:

In this viewpoint Bill Betzen claims that in an open adoption, birth parents and adoptive parents join together out of interest for the child. What is one objection that someone might raise to open adoption that argues against it being in the interest of the child?

Open Adoption Is Not Always the Best Policy

Lisa Hunt Warren

"'Adoption' involves one set of parents becoming the very real parents of a child."

In the following viewpoint Lisa Hunt Warren argues that open adoption is not best for the adopted child. Warren claims that it is least confusing to an adopted child to have just one mother and one father. She believes that adoption is so difficult because it is, and should be, a severing of ties between the child and the birth parent. Warren claims that those who are in favor of open adoption are not adequately focusing on the interests of the adopted child. Warren is a writer and an adoptive mother to one of her three children.

AS YOU READ, CONSIDER THE FOLLOWING QUESTIONS:

1. What kind of harm does the author believe would result from a biological mother calling, visiting, or sending photos to her child given up for adoption?
2. What does Warren say about the worry that an adopted child does not have enough information without contact with a birth parent?
3. In what way does the author claim that contact from a birth mother would have gotten in the way of her mothering?

Lisa Hunt Warren, "Considerations in Choosing Open Adoption," *Helium*, March 6, 2008. www.helium.com. Reproduced by permission.

I didn't have the option of an open adoption when my son was placed with me permanently, so not having that option made me ask myself whether my son was missing something he should have. He came to me after he was removed from the home of the biological mother and after he had sustained a skull fracture for which he was hospitalized and that healed. Once when I asked a social worker a question that led her to realize I was trying to put myself in the biological mother's place she said to me, "You can't do that. She is so different from you there is no way you can put yourself in her place." I later learned that aside from any history of child abuse, the biological mother was said to be "of limited mental capacity". I was told that there was a live-in boyfriend and a question of whether the baby was his and a few other young children that were in one place or another. I haven't described the extent of what I had been told, but this is an example of the truth that I needed to find a way to—at one point in his life or another—share with my son.

Creating Normalcy

When he was very little I was very aware of wanting him to feel like "all the other kids". I did, after all, have two biological children and was particularly aware of my desire to make sure he didn't feel different. When he asked about where babies come from I took advantage of the opportunity to tell him that ladies have babies, and, I added, usually when a lady has a baby she brings the baby home and is his mother; but sometimes if a lady knows she doesn't know how to be a mother or can't take care of a baby the right way she may ask another lady to be the baby's mother. This was my story, and I stuck to it for a good, long,

FAST FACT

Not all agreements about ongoing contact with birth parents are court enforceable, but some states have created legal statues for a formalized agreement known as an Enforceable Contact Agreements (ECA).

time. I reasoned that the normal thing for children is to have one mother and one father at one time. I believed, too, that even if there were the chance to have an open arrangement with this biological mother what that would do would be to put a face on someone who was not to him, at that time, more than a story. Later he would, of course, realize that the "story" had a real person attached to it, but when he was little the story was enough to explain where he came from, and that's all some five-year-olds are interested in.

I reasoned, too, that having an open adoption situation where the biological mother visited or called and where pictures were sent on a regular basis would make an adoption feel like unpaid foster care, besides possibly adding a confusing element to a young child's identity and understanding that he, like everyone else, has just one mother. While I did not change his first name (although I added my father's name as a middle name), and while I certainly admired the golden curls he had inherited from one of the biological parents, there was only so much acknowledgement of her contribution AT THAT TIME that I thought was right if I were to raise a secure child who didn't feel different from his siblings or friends. My plan was not to try to deny him the chance to meet this person someday. I just wanted him to have the very normal, mother/father/three kids/one dog/one cat, family in which to grow, hopefully, secure and well adjusted and able to deal with any issues related to having been adopted once he was mature enough.

Also, although this may sound awfully cold-hearted, I've always believed that the very definition of "adoption" involves one set of parents becoming the very real parents of a child; and in order to have that sacred relationship be what all parent/child relationships are. In other words, if adoption gets watered down to resemble unpaid foster care, the nature of adoption does get completely changed. Whether or not an adoptive relationship can be of equal intensity and strength and bonding when there is a part-time, other mother, who shows up at Christmas time is a question people need to seriously consider. The idea that "there's room for everyone" may not, in reality, hold true when it comes to a child's view of the person who is his mother.

Openness Complicates

My heart has always broken for all biological mothers who give us their children for adoption, but I've always believed that the cold, hard, and even horrible, reality of adoption is that all ties are cut. That is the very thing that makes placing a child for adoption such an awful and difficult thing for biological mothers, but my belief has always

Some opponents of open adoption feel that having relationships with two sets of parents can be detrimental to a child's development.

been if a mother wants to keep in touch with her child she should not be placing him for adoption at all. When the argument in favor of open adoption is aimed at any benefits to the child, I'm not sure that there are benefits; and if there are they may not be worth the complications and even compromises of the child's chance to have what all children tend to see as "normal"—one mother and one father.

When my son was a little past twenty-one years old he received a letter from people who arrange reunions between adopted children and their biological mothers. He told me he wasn't going to "bother" because he wasn't "interested", and I asked him if he would at least call the woman who contacted him and tell her to tell the biological mother he is ok. I told him she deserves at least that much. He eventually agreed to meet his biological mother and some biological family members, and it did throw him a little to discover some of the ugly facts surrounding his beginnings. My bond with my son, however, is as strong as they come; and just as I had picked up the pieces after his rough beginnings, I embarked 21 years later on efforts to help pick up the pieces after his reunion. I'm not an adopted child, and there's a whole lot I don't know about my own "roots" beyond my parents. I've lived comfortably without a lot of information, and I can't help but believe that adopted people, too, could live comfortably without some information IF they have been raised in a way that has not caused them to overemphasize the importance of that information.

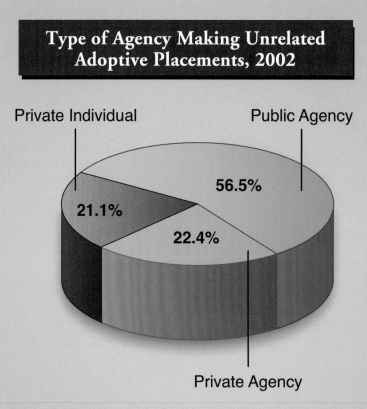

Type of Agency Making Unrelated Adoptive Placements, 2002

Private Individual

Public Agency

56.5%

21.1%

22.4%

Private Agency

Taken from: Paul Placek, "National Adoption Data," in *Adoption Factbook IV*, eds. Thomas C. Atwood, Lee A. Allen, and Virginia C. Ravenel. Alexandria, VA: National Council for Adoption, 2007, p. 36. Available at www.adoptioncouncil.org/documents/AdoptionFactbookIV.pdf.

I am in favor of sharing some information with even the youngest adopted child, and I'm in favor of sharing more information as the child grows. Doing this can help prepare a child for the reunion that probably will, and should, take place. To that extent, I'm not in favor of "deep, dark, secrets" sealed in files somewhere. When it comes, however, to a child's having "Mary, who visits" and "Mommy who I live with", I just think it robs a child of an innocence and normal childhood. If the arrangement will be that the child never knows that "Aunt Mary" is his biological mother, then the only point in having "Mary" come around or call wouldn't be to give the child knowledge of his whole story but, instead, just to let "Aunt Mary" keep in touch with her biological child, and that may be good for "Aunt Mary" but when reunion time comes the child may be thrown more for a loop than the child who meets a stranger who introduces herself as his biological mother.

What Is Best for the Child

Finally: I adopted my son because I wanted him, and there has never been one second of the last 30 years when I allowed myself to think about what I offered him rather than the joy and love he brought into my life. Still, with every child we have we devote an incredibly amount of love, worry, thought, and nurturing. With an adopted child there can be a little extra thought and planning involved because of the circumstances. I was able to raise my son with his siblings, who happen to be my biological children, as my own because there was no other mother in the picture. I could not have done an equally good job of that if a biological mother were sending me mail and calling and expecting pictures. It may sound unreasonable, but there is something in my maternal instinct that would not be capable of sustaining the quality of the bond I share with all three of my kids if the dynamics had been changed.

People sometimes seem to forget that the adoptive mother isn't just someone who was blessed with a child, but she is often someone required to figure out how to build that unshakable bond even with some of the "holes" that can threaten the adoptive bond. She can also be someone who is left to pick up the pieces when a child's beginnings affect something like his ability to learn once he gets to school. My belief is that I could not have done as good a job FOR my son (not me) under an open adoption arrangement; and while my heart goes out to biological mothers who give up their babies, I think adoptive mothers should have the right and responsibility to do the best job possible—and there is at least the possiblity that closed adoption may allow adoptive mothers to do just that.

EVALUATING THE AUTHORS' ARGUMENTS:

In this viewpoint Lisa Hunt Warren suggests that central to the question of open adoption is the interests of the child, as does the author of the previous viewpoint, Bill Betzen. Explain why it is that Warren and Betzen reach such different conclusions.

Viewpoint

5

More Foster Children Should Be Placed in Adoptive Homes

Jennifer Roback Morse

"Adoption removes a child from the foster-care system."

In the following viewpoint Jennifer Roback Morse argues that children in foster care need to be adopted more swiftly. Appealing to the example of a foster child who died in foster care, Morse claims that the child could have been saved if the child welfare system had taken the steps to ensure his adoption. Morse is a research fellow at the Acton Institute for the Study of Religion and Liberty, a regular columnist for the *National Catholic Register*, the parent of an adopted child, and a foster parent.

AS YOU READ, CONSIDER THE FOLLOWING QUESTIONS:
1. According to Morse, what killed two-year-old Malachi?
2. Why did Malachi's birth parents not release him to be adopted, according to the author?
3. The author believes that rather than prioritizing the needs of vulnerable children to be adopted, the child welfare system puts a higher priority on what?

Jennifer Roback Morse, "Who Killed Malachi?" *National Review Online*, July 26, 2007. Reproduced by permission of the author.

"**F**amily Buries Toddler" read the headline in the *San Diego Union-Tribune*. Police arrested the child's foster mother, on suspicion of her perpetrating the massive brain injuries which caused the two-year-old's death. But the people really responsible for the child's demise will never be arrested. Although it is customary to blame the incompetence of the foster-care system for a senseless death like this, foster care per se did not kill Malachi. The child welfare system's unwillingness to terminate parental rights killed him.

Child Welfare System Responsible

According to the *Union-Tribune*, the facts are these:

> Malachi Jermaine McBride-Roberts' life was brief and difficult. He was born to a teenage mother living in foster care. After she ran away, he was sent to live with another foster family. . . .
>
> "This would not have happened had he been in my care," said the boy's 23 year old father.

A normal person might well ask, "Why, then, sir, was he not in your care?" The answer is that the system does not require birth parents to "fish or cut bait." The system does not insist that birth parents either take responsibility for the child, or release him to someone who will, namely, adoptive parents. Some birth parents consider the best of all worlds to be keeping parental rights, seeing the child once in a while, but letting someone else do the hands-on child-care work. Unfortunately, the system enables, rather than discourages this posture.

The situation of the birth mother is even more striking. Keshia Roberts, raised in foster care from the time she was 9 months old, was 16 when she gave birth to Malachi. . . . For the first 16 months of Malachi's life, Eddtwanna Starks was his foster mother. She also cared for the boy's mother. But the living arrangements fell apart earlier this year [2007].

> ## FAST FACT
>
> The U.S. Department of Health and Human Services reports that in 2005, eight hundred thousand children were in the foster care system, and of these, over one hundred thousand were waiting to be adopted.

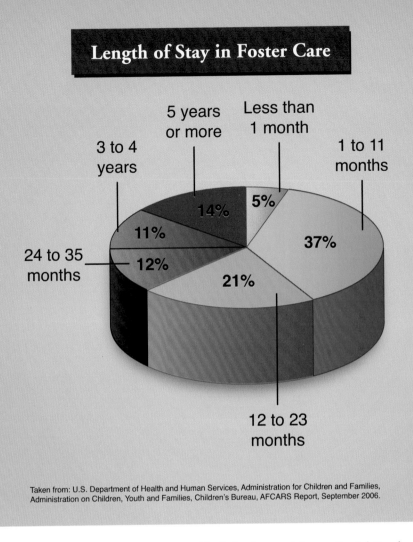

Length of Stay in Foster Care

5 years or more — 14%

Less than 1 month — 5%

3 to 4 years — 11%

1 to 11 months — 37%

24 to 35 months — 12%

12 to 23 months — 21%

Taken from: U.S. Department of Health and Human Services, Administration for Children and Families, Administration on Children, Youth and Families, Children's Bureau, AFCARS Report, September 2006.

"Keshia suddenly ran away and left the boy with me," said Starks, 32. Without the mother to help, Starks said she couldn't give the boy the care he needed. She had other children living with her.

That's when Malachi was placed with the foster mother who is charged with murdering him.

Adoption Is the Solution

Adoption removes a child from the foster-care system. Adoptive parents become accountable for a child in a way that the bureaucratic government agency never can be. Adopted children do better than the children of single mothers. And even the average child of an average single mother has far better life chances than a child in foster care.

Some feel that the death of two-year-old Malachi Jermaine McBride-Roberts could have been prevented if the child welfare system had taken steps to ensure his adoption.

I have no wish to pile on these grieving young parents. But the simple truth is that if they had released their son for adoption at birth, he would almost certainly be alive and thriving today.

His 16-year-old mother had then and has now, no means of supporting herself. She was not then and is not now, married to the child's father. In any sane social universe, the adults around this mother and child would have gently advised her to place him for adoption, for his own good.

Tragically for vulnerable children, the system puts a higher priority on protecting the due-process rights of birth mothers. I formed this opinion during the three years I was a foster parent in San Diego County. I suspect San Diego is typical, not exceptional. Although California law requires infants to be "fast-tracked" for permanent placement, attorneys and judges don't want their decisions overturned on appeal. They have stronger incentives to cover all the legal procedural bases, than to make good placement decisions. By the time the child is finally available for adoption, he may be no longer adoptable.

Most likely, no one suggested adoption to Malachi's mother. She probably had a court-appointed, taxpayer-funded attorney to help her maintain her parental rights, rights she was in no position to actually exercise. All she could do with her rights is to block a family from adopting him.

So who killed Malachi? The attorneys and social workers who helped his mother keep her parental rights killed him. The law that simultaneously instructs social workers to protect children and reunify "families," killed Malachi.

And none of those guilty parties will ever be held accountable for anything.

EVALUATING THE AUTHOR'S ARGUMENTS:

In this viewpoint Jennifer Roback Morse argues that the child welfare system needs to be reformed to enable children to be adopted more swiftly. What would be a reasonable amount of time to allow parents to regain full parental rights before termination to make way for adoption? Explain your answer.

Foster Children Should Not Always Be Placed in Adoptive Homes

New York Amsterdam News

"They've been moved around so much, they say, that adoption seems confining."

In the following viewpoint the *New York Amsterdam News* supports the view that not all children in foster care want to be adopted. Recounting the stories of two children in foster care, eighteen-year-old Jai and sixteen-year-old Pui-nu, two personal views are given that support the view that adoption may not always be best for the children in foster care. The *New York Amsterdam News* is a weekly newspaper aimed at the African American community of New York since 1909.

AS YOU READ, CONSIDER THE FOLLOWING QUESTIONS:
1. According to eighteen-year-old Jai, why did she choose to be in foster care over adoption, when given the option?
2. What is the purpose of the Theater for Action in the lives of foster care children of New York?
3. What is Pui-nu's view of adults that explains the preference not to be adopted?

New York City's recent campaign to push kids out of foster care and into adoptive families will affect 3,500 kids in the city. Two of the kids CPL [Children's PressLine] interviewed at the Jewish Child Care Association's Theater for Action, a foster-care theater program, would rather stay in foster care than be adopted. They've been moved around so much, they say, that adoption seems confining.

Jai's View

Jai, 18: I've been a foster kid since I was four years old. My mom abuses crack cocaine, heroin and is also a prostitute.

I don't remember her being a bad mom. I just remember being in the streets a lot, walking around outside. I don't remember her using drugs in front of me or nothing.

I feel as though foster care has changed my life in a positive way. If it wasn't for foster care I'd probably be using drugs or pregnant. It gave me a stable home, a chance to get an education and a better life. It's been good because I'm with a foster mother that had experience raising children; my mother really didn't know how to raise me.

When I was 16 they gave me the option to either be adopted or to be in foster care. I chose to be in foster care because it's better. You have more chances [to find the right family]. If you get adopted, that's it; that's the end of it. Going back to my parents was never an option for me, because my mother doesn't want me back.

Because my mother did drugs, I stayed away from drugs my whole life because I was kind of scared. I'm so terrified of drugs.

> **FAST FACT**
>
> According to Children's Rights, approximately twenty thousand children "age out" of the foster care system annually when they reach the age of eighteen, without returning home to families or being adopted.

When I was little they gave me away. My mother gave me to my grandmother because she was on drugs and had another boy. That boy was found in a deserted car. Somebody called the police and they took him away. They found out he had a sister, so they took me away

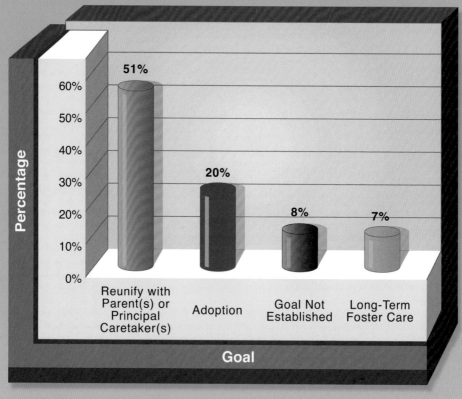

Case Goals of Children in Foster Care

51%

60%

50%

40%

30%   20%

20%   8%   7%

10%

0%

Percentage

Reunify with
Parent(s) or
Principal
Caretaker(s)

Adoption

Goal Not
Established

Long-Term
Foster Care

Goal

Taken from: U.S. Department of Health and Human Services, Administration for Children and Families,
Administration on Children, Youth and Families, Children's Bureau, AFCARS Report, September 2006.

too. My other brother was living with my father. They didn't take him until he was older. Then my mother had another boy while she was locked up, and they took him away. She had a girl too, but they didn't take her.

I'm graduating in January. I'm currently on the honor role, representing for the smart geeks.

Right now I really don't want children. I feel like I'm too young. When I'm older, I think I will have a few buckaroos of my own.

The Theater for Action

We do [the plays in Theater for Action] for foster children in the system. We're the audience and the actors. It's good to get a message across that we're not alone. All of us have problems. It's not like someone is going to laugh at you; we've all been there.

[The play we're doing now] is about this girl who was in foster care for a few years. She got attached to her foster family, but she was going home. She was happy to be going home, but when she got there . . . there were a lot of conflicts. It was a mess. The grandmother was still drinking and the mother had an attitude. But when she went back to her foster mother, somebody replaced her spot in the bed. There was no room for her. She ended up overdosing and committing suicide. In the end we asked people to join us onstage and replace characters that were being mistreated, and so they could fix the ending of the story.

It's weird working with the moms that had their children removed and you're a child that's been removed.

It helps us to cope. The rehearsals take up a lot of time, and you grow a bond with these people that you didn't know. You have to

Proponents of foster care say that many foster children do not want to be adopted because it can feel confining.

put yourself out there. You have to put your heart and soul out there. When you're acting, you're telling your story. If you were telling someone else's story it would be different. But you're telling your story.

Pui-nu's View

Pui-nu, 16: My dad's an alcoholic. My mom is a ho. I've been in the foster care since March, but my dad has been drinking my whole life. My foster parent is my aunt.

I want to have kids so that I can treat them the way I never got love from my mom. I would treat them different. I know I'll spoil them, though.

Before [Theater for Action], all I did was stay home, go to sleep and watch TV. That was my daily routine. I OD'd twice on alcohol. The second time I was in the hospital and my dad came to get me a day later with alcohol on his breath. . . . I've been in [foster care] ever since.

I've moved a lot. That's the reason I don't trust adults. Once you think you're in a stable place, they take you out. Once you think you can trust an adult, you're gone.

EVALUATING THE AUTHORS' ARGUMENTS:

In this viewpoint the *New York Amsterdam News* claims that not all children want to be adopted by recounting the views of two foster children. What do you think the author of the previous viewpoint, Jennifer Roback Morse, would say about these teenagers' views on adoption?

Facts About Adoption

Editors' note: These facts can be used in reports or papers to reinforce or add credibility when making important points or claims.

Legal Issues
- Adoption is the legal act of transferring parental rights and responsibilities to an individual (or individuals) who is not the biological parent.
- Legally, there is no difference between a parent by birth and a parent created by legal adoption.
- Even in a so-called open adoption, legal rights of guardianship of the birth parent are terminated.

Types of Adoption
- Foster care adoption is the adoption of children in state care whose parents have had their parental rights terminated for a variety of reasons. Adoption is arranged by state child welfare agencies or by private agencies under contract with the states.
- Private adoption occurs with or without an adoption agency. Adoption agencies may be nonprofit or for-profit and are licensed by the state. Independent adoptions, performed without an agency, often use an attorney to help with the agreement between the birth parents and the adoptive parent(s).
- International adoptions, usually arranged through adoption agencies, are adoptions that occur between countries.
- Transracial adoption refers to an adoption where an adopted child is of a different race than that of the adoptive parent(s).

Adoption Statistics
- As of the 2000 U.S. Census, there were 1.5 million adopted children under the age of eighteen in the United States, over 2 percent of all U.S. children.
- While annual adoptions in the United States are not comprehensively compiled, the National Center for State Courts estimates that approximately 40 percent of all adoptions are stepparent

adoptions, and 15 percent of adoptions are adoptions out of foster care.

- According to a study by the National Council for Adoption, within the United States in 2002 there were 130,269 domestic adoptions and 21,063 intercountry adoptions. Among the domestic adoptions, 76,013 were adoptions between otherwise unrelated individuals (that is, not grandparents, etc.).
- The National Council for Adoption reports that in 2002, 57 percent of unrelated domestic adoptions were performed by public agencies, 22 percent by private agencies, and 21 percent by private individuals.
- The United States Children's Bureau estimates that for each of the years from 2002 to 2006, just over 50,000 children were adopted from foster care, leaving approximately 130,000 each year waiting to be adopted.
- According to a study by the National Council for Adoption, the number of domestic adoptions grew by over 20 percent from 1996 (108,463) to 2002, whereas the number of intercountry adoptions grew by 86 percent from 11,303 intercountry adoptions in 1996.
- In recent years the numbers of international adoptions and foster care adoptions have risen significantly.
- The cost to adopt can range from as little as nothing, in adoptions from the foster care system, to over thirty thousand dollars for some private adoptions and international adoptions.

Adoption Language

- Proponents of Respectful Adoption Language, created in the 1970s, seek to use terms that present adoption in a positive light, with a focus on respecting the role of the adoptive parents. Preferred terms include:
  1. *birth* parent, instead of *real* parent or *natural* parent, which imply the adoptive parent is either not real or unnatural.
  2. *child,* instead of *adopted child,* which implies the adoptive child is not, to the adoptive parent, one's own.
  3. *placed* for adoption, instead of *given up* for adoption, which is more emotionally charged.

- Proponents of Honest Adoption Language, with a greater focus on how the language affects the mother who gives birth, prefers the following language:
  1. *natural* or *first* mother, rather than *birth* mother, to denote the enduring bond between mother and child, as well as to avoid limiting the mother's role to that of simply reproduction.
  2. *natural* child or *child of one's own,* instead of *birth* child, which implies there is no connection to the child other than at birth.
  3. *surrendered* for adoption or *lost* to adoption, rather than *placed,* in order not to deny the emotional effect of separation.

Organizations to Contact

The editors have compiled the following list of organizations concerned with the issues debated in this book. The descriptions are derived from materials provided by the organizations. All have publications or information available for interested readers. The list was compiled on the date of publication of the present volume; the information provided here may change. Be aware that many organizations take several weeks or longer to respond to inquiries, so allow as much time as possible.

Abolish Adoption
PO Box 401, Palm Desert, CA 92261
e-mail: info@abolishadoption.com
Web site: www.abolishadoption.com

Abolish Adoption is an organization that petitions to end the practice of adoption. Abolish Adoption lobbies, protests, petitions, and sues for open birth and adoption records. Its publications include *The Ultimate Search Book: Worldwide Adoption, Genealogy and Other Search Secrets* by Lori Carangelo.

Alternative Family Matters
PO Box 390618, Cambridge, MA 02139
(617) 576-6788
e-mail: jenifer@altenativefamilies.org
Web site: www.alternativefamilies.org

Alternative Family Matters is an agency that assists lesbians, gay men, bisexuals, and transgendered people (LGBTs) who want to have children through adoption, artificial insemination, or surrogacy. The agency also educates the medical community to better understand and serve LGBT-headed families. Alternative Family Matters created the Conception Connection Registry and Counseling Service, which specializes in facilitating parenting arrangements between otherwise unrelated men and women who want to have children together.

American Adoption Congress (AAC)
PO Box 42730, Washington, DC 20015
(202) 483-3399
Web site: www.americanadoptioncongress.org

The AAC is an educational network that promotes openness and honesty in adoption. It advocates adoption reform, including open adoption records. The AAC publishes the quarterly *Decree* and also has position statements available on its Web site.

Bastard Nation
PO Box 1469, Edmond, OK 73083-1469
(415) 704-3166
e-mail: bn@bastards.org
Web site: www.bastards.org

Bastard Nation advocates for the civil and human rights of adult citizens who were adopted as children. The organization campaigns for the access of birth and adoption records. Bastard Nation's publications include *The Basic Bastard,* a book of articles on adoptee rights, and the *Bastard Quarterly* newsletter.

Child Welfare Information Gateway
1250 Maryland Ave. SW, 8th Flr., Washington, DC 20024
(800) 394-3366
e-mail: info@childwelfare.gov
Web site: www.childwelfare.gov

The Child Welfare Information Gateway is a service of the Children's Bureau in the Administration for Children and Families, part of the U.S. Department of Health and Human Services. The Child Welfare Information Gateway promotes the safety, permanency, and well-being of children and families by connecting child welfare, adoption, and related professionals to essential information. Resources available at the Web site include the National Foster Care and Adoption Directory.

Child Welfare League of America (CWLA)
2345 Crystal Dr., Ste. 250, Arlington, VA 22202
(703) 412-2400 • fax: (703) 412-2401
Web site: www.cwla.org

The CWLA is an association of hundreds of public and private non-profit agencies that assist abused and neglected children. The association promotes standards of excellence in adoption services. The CWLA publishes the *Children's Voice* magazine and the *Child Welfare* journal.

Concerned United Birthparents (CUB)

PO Box 503475, San Diego, CA 92150-3475
(800) 822-2777 • fax: (858) 712-3317
e-mail: info@cubirthparents.org
Web site: www.cubirthparents.org

CUB is a nonprofit organization providing support for family members separated by adoption. CUB has support groups for birth parents and seeks to educate the public about the lifelong impact on all who are touched by adoption. CUB publishes a newsletter, *CUB Communicator,* and also has available at its Web site the booklet *What You Should KNOW If You're Considering Adoption for Your Baby.*

Dave Thomas Foundation for Adoption

4150 Tuller Rd., Ste. 204, Dublin, OH 43017
(800) 275-3832
e-mail: info@davethomasfoundation.org
Web site: www.davethomasfoundation.org

The Dave Thomas Foundation for Adoption works to increase the number of adoptions of waiting children in foster care in North America. The foundation funds adoption recruiters who focus on the adoption of children in foster care and leads the National Adoption Day, a collaborative national effort to raise awareness about children in foster care waiting to be adopted. Publications include *A Child Is Waiting: A Beginner's Guide to Adoption* and the *National Foster Care Adoption Attitudes Survey.*

Evan B. Donaldson Adoption Institute

120 East Thirty-eighth St., New York, NY 10016
(212) 925-4089 • fax: (775) 796-6592
e-mail: info@adoptioninstitute.org
Web site: www.adoptioninstitute.org

The Even B. Donaldson Adoption Institute is a nonprofit organization devoted to improving adoption policy and practice. The institute conducts research, offers education, promotes legal reforms, and works to change policy. There are numerous publications, presentations, and conference proceedings available at their Web site, including the white paper *Safeguarding the Rights and Well-Being of Birthparents in the Adoption Process.*

Families for Private Adoption (FPA)

PO Box 6375, Washington, DC 20015-0375
(202) 722-0338
e-mail: info@ffpa.org
Web site: www.ffpa.org

FPA is an adoption support and education group that advocates and encourages private (nonagency) adoption. FPA hosts educational programs for couples seeking to adopt. The group publishes a newsletter and a guide to successful adoption, the *Adoption Book.*

Institute for Adoption Information (IAI)

409 Dewey St., Bennington, VT 05201
(802) 442-2845
e-mail: info@adoptioninformationinstitute.org
Web site: www.adoptioninformationinstitute.org

The IAI is a nonprofit organization of adoptees, birth parents, adoptive parents, adoption professionals, and others who have united to enhance the understanding of adoption. The institute advocates for balanced, accurate coverage of adoption in news and entertainment media. The IAI's publications include the brochure *Why It Is Important to Understand Adoption.*

National Adoption Center (NAC)

1500 Walnut St., Ste. 701, Philadelphia, PA 19102
(800) 862-3678
e-mail: nac@adopt.org
Web site: www.adopt.org

The NAC expands adoption opportunities for children living in foster care throughout the United States. The center sponsors the Wednesday's Child Web site, which has photos and descriptions of children available for adoption. The NAC publishes the online magazine *NACzine.*

National American Council on Adoptable Children (NACAC)

970 Raymond Ave, Ste. 106, St. Paul, MN 55114
(651) 644-3036 • fax: (65l) 644-9848
e-mail: info@nacac.org
Web site: www.nacac.org

The NACAC promotes and supports permanent families for children and youth in the United States and Canada who are in foster care and who have special needs. The NACAC provides education and advocacy for adoption and offers leadership training to parents to help create and enhance support groups. The NACAC publishes a quarterly newsletter, *Adoptalk.*

National Council for Adoption (NCFA)

225 N. Washington St., Alexandria, VA 22314-2561
(703) 299-6633 • fax: (703) 299-6004
e-mail: ncfa@adoptioncouncil.org
Web site: www.adoptioncouncil.org

The NCFA is a research, education, and advocacy organization whose mission is to promote the well-being of children, birth parents, and adoptive families. As part of its work promoting sound adoption policies, the NCFA provides strategic policy briefs and expert testimony at legislative hearings. The NCFA publishes the *Adoption Factbook IV,* a comprehensive source of adoption facts and statistics.

RainbowKids

PO Box 202, Harvey, LA 70059
e-mail: martha@rainbowkids.com
Web site: www.rainbowkids.com

RainbowKids is an adoption advocacy Web site, helping people adopt from multiple countries. RainbowKids offers education about international adoption, support during the adoption process, and resources to assist with a newly adopted child. RainbowKids publishes an online adoption advocacy magazine monthly.

For Further Reading

Books

Dorow, Sara. *Transnational Adoption: A Cultural Economy of Race, Gender, and Kinship.* New York: NYU Press, 2006. A professor of sociology studies the largest contemporary intercountry adoption program, between China and the United States. The author describes the ways that parents construct the cultural and racial identities of adopted children.

Duxbury, Micky. *Making Room in Our Hearts: Keeping Family Ties Through Open Adoption.* New York: Routledge, 2006. Based on interviews with more than one hundred adopted children, birth and adoptive parents, extended families, professionals, and experts, this firsthand look at adoption supports the view that open adoption helps children to develop stronger identities.

Fogg-Davis, Hawley. *The Ethics of Transracial Adoption.* Syracuse, NY: Cornell University Press, 2002. A professor of political science carves out a middle ground in the debate about transracial adoption, arguing that race should not be a barrier to adoption but neither should it be ignored.

Garner, Abigail. *Families Like Mine: Children of Gay Parents Tell It Like It Is.* New York: HarperCollins, 2005. A daughter of a gay father, drawing on interviews with other sons and daughters of gay, lesbian, bisexual, and transgender parents, addresses topics such as homophobia, coparenting, and sexuality.

Kennedy, Randall. *Interracial Intimacies: Sex, Marriage, Identity, and Adoption.* New York: Pantheon, 2003. A Harvard law professor examines the history of interracial relationships. The author explores how social attitudes have affected the social policy on a variety of issues, including interracial adoption.

Mallon, Gerald P. *Lesbian and Gay Foster and Adoptive Parents.* Arlington, VA: CWLA, 2006. The author contends that gay and lesbian people are an underused resource in adoption because of stereotypes, prejudices, and legislation that make it difficult for them to foster or adopt.

Melosh, Barbara. *Strangers and Kin: The American Way of Adoption.* Cambridge, MA: Harvard University Press, 2006. A professor of English and history explores the history of adoption in the United States, showing how various social changes, such as the sexual revolution, have changed attitudes toward adoption.

Nelson-Erichsen, Jean. *Inside the Adoption Agency: Understanding Intercountry Adoption in the Era of the Hague Convention.* Bloomington, IN: iUniverse, 2007. A leading pioneer of intercountry adoption explains the history of intercountry adoption and argues that the Hague Convention on the Protection of Children and Co-operation in Respect of Intercountry Adoption has improved the process.

Patton, Sandra. *Birthmarks: Transracial Adoption in Contemporary America.* New York: New York University Press, 2000. A professor of women's studies explores the controversial issue of transracial adoption. Neither an argument for nor against transracial adoption, the author counters the view of transracial adoption as a panacea to the so-called epidemic of illegitimacy.

Pertman, Adam. *Adoption Nation: How the Adoption Revolution Is Transforming America.* New York: Basic Books, 2001. The author takes a broad look at open adoption, international adoption, and multiracial adoption, arguing that adoption is transforming American culture and the meaning of family.

Rauhala, Ann. *The Lucky Ones: Our Stories of Adopting Children from China.* Toronto: ECW, 2008. Various families share their stories of adopting children from China. The stories of the girls adopted from China are stories of both hope and dislocation.

Rothman, Barbara Katz. *Weaving a Family: Untangling Race and Adoption.* Boston: Beacon, 2005. A professor of sociology and white mother of a black child considers the issues at the intersection of race and family. The growing number of families formed by interracial adoption are radically changing the face of the American family.

Rush, Sharon. *Loving Across the Color Line: A White Adoptive Mother Learns About Race.* Lanham, MD: Rowman & Littlefield, 2000. A civil rights lawyer and professor of law offers a memoir of interracial adoption. As a white woman with a black daughter, the author claims the devastation of racism is much greater than most whites can imagine.

Snow, Judith E. *How It Feels to Have a Lesbian or Gay Parent: A Book by Kids for Kids of All Ages.* New York: Harrington Park, 2004. By kids for kids, this book takes a look at the effect on children of learning of their parents' homosexual sexual orientation, with recurring themes of prejudice, conflict, adaptation, and tolerance.

Volkman, Toby Alice, ed. *Cultures of Transnational Adoption.* Duke University Press, 2005. Multiple contributors, including adoptive parents, discuss how transnational adoption creates and transforms cultures. Questions are raised on topics such as race, kinship, biology, and belonging.

Periodicals

Atwood, Thomas. "The Child's Best Interests: Malawi's Bureaucratic Adoption Nightmare," *Washington Times,* October 25, 2006.

Cameron, Paul. "Yes: The Conclusions of the American Academy of Pediatrics Are Not to Be Believed," *Insight on the News,* February 17, 2004.

Cho, Stephanie, and Kim So Yung. "Abductees Speak: Transracial Adoptees Take on the Adoption Agencies," *Eurasian Nation,* June 2003.

Colorlines Magazine. "Making a Family: Adoption Is a Pressing Racial Issue as More Children of Color Are Adopted by White Parents," July–August 2006.

Cowan, Alyssa Burrell. "New Strategies to Promote the Adoption of Older Children out of Foster Care," *Children and Youth Services Review,* November 2004.

CQ Researcher. "Disputed Studies Give Gay Parents Good Marks," September 5, 2003.

Creamer, Anita. "Adoption's a Test of Patience," *Sacramento Bee,* December 19, 2007.

Current Health 2, A Weekly Reader Publication. "We Are a Family," March 2008.

Dejevsky, Mary. "Why I Support Churches on Gay Adoption," *Independent*, January 25, 2007.

Dusky, Lorraine. "Adoptees Have Right to Know Who They Are," *Albany Times Union*, June 1, 2003.

Edelhart, Courtenay. "One Family, Two Worlds," *Indianapolis Star*, December 6, 2004.

Ferguson, Sue. "Hard-Sell Adoption," *Maclean's*, July 26, 2004.

Fisher, Ann. "Who Adopts Child More Important than Where," *Columbus Dispatch*, November 5, 2007.

Foston, Nikitta A. "Small Miracles: New Hope for Black Adoptions," *Ebony*, November 2003.

Goodman, Ellen. "Gay Adoption's Biggest Advantage," *Buffalo News*, March 27, 2006.

Griffith, Ezra E.H., and Rachel L. Bergeron. "Cultural Stereotypes Die Hard: The Case of Transracial Adoption," *Journal of the American Academy of Psychiatry and Law*, September 1, 2006.

Hamilton, Anita. "When Foster Teens Find a Home," *Time*, June 5, 2006.

Helper, Alexandra N. "The 'Motherless' Child: Some Issues in Adoption," *Psychiatric Times*, February 1, 2005.

Henman, Jessica. "Giving Pregnant Teens Another Option: Teaching About Adoption," *International Journal of Childbirth Education*, June 2005.

Larsen, Elizabeth. "Did I Steal My Daughter? The Answers Are Never Easy When You Enter the Labyrinth of Global Adoption," *Mother Jones*, November–December 2007.

Laurance, Jeremy. "Is It Exploitation to Adopt Children from the Developing World?" *Independent*, October 6, 2006.

McClelland, Susan. "From Darfur, with Love," *Canadian Living*, February 2008.

National Association of Black Social Workers. "Preserving Families of African Ancestry," January 10, 2003. www.nabsw.org.

O'Shea, Brendan C. "Adoption Law Must Respect Birth Parents' Wishes," *Albany Times Union*, June 8, 2003.

Padgett, Tim. "Gay Family Values," *Time,* July 16, 2007.

Poole, Sheila M. "Canadians Look South to Adopt Black Kids," *Atlanta Journal-Constitution,* August 24, 2004.

Rauschart, Lisa. "Not 'Unadoptable': New Effort to Find Homes for Older Foster Children," *World & I,* August 2004.

Richardson, Nicole Marie. "Adopt a Child: Black Children Flood the Foster Care System, *Black Enterprise,* May 2008.

Russell, Beth Nonte. "The Mystery of China's Orphans," *International Herald Tribune,* February 2, 2007.

Ryan, Scott D., Sue Pearlmutter, and Victor Groza. "Coming Out of the Closet: Opening Agencies to Gay and Lesbian Adoptive Parents," *Social Work,* January 2004.

San Jose Mercury News. "Global Adoption Reform Is Long Overdue," December 17, 2007.

Sanchez, Julian. "All Happy Families: The Looming Battle over Gay Parenting," *Reason,* August/September 2005.

Savage, Dan. "Is No Adoption Really Better than a Gay Adoption?" *New York Times,* September 8, 2001.

Schmidt, Ellie Bradsher, and Barbara Pearson. "Adoption Without Boundaries," *Children's Voice Magazine,* May–June 2007.

St. Louis Post-Dispatch. "The Adoption Morass," August 13, 2007.

Stamato, Linda. "Let Adoptees Find Biological Identity," *Star-Ledger,* September 16, 2007.

Trust, Carol J., and Mark Gianino. "Bad-Faith Pitch for Bigotry," *Boston Herald,* March 11, 2006.

USA Today Magazine. "Adoption More Open for Gays and Lesbians," April 2003.

Wingert, Pat. "When There's No Place Like Home," *Newsweek International,* February 4, 2008.

Zibart, Rosemary. "Teens Wanted: Adopt an Adolescent? Yes, There Are Families Crazy and Loving Enough to Take That On," *Time,* April 4, 2005.

Web Sites

ABCAdoptions.com (www.abcadoptions.com). This Web site provides adoption information, resources, and services to future birth mothers, prospective adoptive parents, and adoption professionals.

AdoptUsKids.org (www.adoptuskids.org). AdoptUsKids.org is a Web site for connecting foster and adoptive families with waiting foster children throughout the United States, offering pictures and information about waiting children, as well as resources on adoption.

Insight: Open Adoption Resources and Support (www.openadoption insight.org). This Web site, not affiliated with any adoption agency or facilitation service, aims to offer information and support for healthy open adoption relationships.

Index

A

Abortion
adoption as alternative to,
21–25
adoption is not alternative
to, 26–30
increase in, 94
reasons for, 29
sex-selection, 32
statistics on, 28

Adopted children
demand for, 58
needs of, 50–51
normalcy for, 105–106
race/ethnicity of, 69
See also Adult adoptees

Adoption
as abortion alternative,
21–25
costs of, 58–59
difficulty of, 24, 28
of foster children,
111–120
gay, 43–53
is not abortion alternative,
26–30
language, 122–123
legal issues, 121
as social good, 11–15
as social ill, 16–20
statistics on, 121–122

stigma of, 29–30
transracial, 54–71
types of, 121
waiting times, 58
See also International
adoption; Open
adoption

Adoption agencies
African American, 68,
69–70
discrimination by, 44–45
fees charged by, 58–59
fraudulent information by,
7–8, 79
open, 98, 103

Adoption industry,
reproductive exploitation
and, 17–18

Adoption records
should be open to
adoptees, 83–88
should not be open,
89–96

Adoption-Link, 55, 56, 62

Adoptions from the Heart,
8

Adoptive families
open adoption benefits,
98–99
open adoption undermines,
93–94

Picture Credits

AFP/Getty Images, 38

AP Images, 13, 20, 46, 75, 82, 87, 91, 102, 119

© Bubbles Photolibrary/Alamy, 60

Cartoon by Nigel Sutherland. www.CartooonStock.com, 18

Nelvin C. Cepeda/San Diego Union Tribune/ZUMA Press, 114

Emmanuel Dunand/AFP/Getty Images, 52

Image copyright Gelpi, 2008. Used under license from Shutterstock. com, 10

Image copyright Htuller, 2008. Used under license from Shutterstock. com, 67

© Richard Levine/Alamy, 42

Orlando Sierra/AFP/Getty Images, 80

Signe Wilkinson Editorial Cartoon © 2006 Signe Wilkinson. All rights reserved. Used with the permission of Signe Wilkinson and the Washington Post Writers Group in conjunction with the Cartoonist Group, 78

© Tom Stewart/Corbis, 27

© 2002 by Jeff Parker, Florida Today and CagleCartoons.com. All rights reserved, 51

Alex Wong/Getty Images, 24

© David Young-Wolff/Alamy, 107

Steve Zmina, 14, 23, 29, 32, 40, 45, 57, 69, 73, 84, 95, 99, 108, 113, 118

Simon Zo/Reuters/Landov, 34